ALSO BY GERALD MARZORATI

A Painter of Darkness

LATE

TO THE

BALL

Age.
Learn.
Fight.
Love.
Play Tennis.
Win.

GERALD
MARZORATI

SCRIBNER

New York London Toronto Sydney New Delhi

SCRIBNER
An Imprint of Simon & Schuster, Inc.
1230 Avenue of the Americas
New York, NY 10020

First Scribner hardcover edition May 2016

SCRIBNER and design are registered trademarks of
The Gale Group, Inc. used under license by Simon & Schuster, Inc.,
the publisher of this work.

For information about special discounts for bulk purchases,
please contact Simon & Schuster Special Sales at 1-866-506-1949
or business@simonandschuster.com.

The Simon & Schuster Speakers Bureau can bring authors to
your live event. For more information or to book an event, contact
the Simon & Schuster Speakers Bureau at 1-866-248-3049
or visit our website at www.simonspeakers.com.

Interior design by Kyle Kabel

Manufactured in the United States of America

1   3   5   7   9   10   8   6   4   2

Library of Congress Cataloguing in Publication data
has been applied for.

ISBN 978-1-4767-3739-3
ISBN 978-1-4767-3743-0 (ebook)

For my sons, Guy and Luca

What do you do if you're sixty-two and you realize all those bodily parts invisible up to now (kidneys, lungs, veins, arteries, brain, intestines, prostate, heart) are about to start making themselves distressingly apparent . . . ?

Here's what happens: you feel excruciatingly how old you are, but in a new way.

Philip Roth, *The Dying Animal*

To toss the ball, to arch my back,
unwind like lightning,
with the stringed surface, from the shoulder
to skim the ball's occiput,
and, lunging, the whistling return
to devastatingly cut short—
the world has not a sweeter pastime . . .
in heaven we shall be playing ball.

Vladimir Nabokov, "The University Poem"

Sometimes, Tom, we have to do a thing in order to find out the reason for it. Sometimes our actions are questions, not answers.

John le Carré, *A Perfect Spy*

LATE TO THE | BALL

1

"Does the court seem small somehow to you?" I asked Kirill. He took a long look. "It does."

But I couldn't figure out why, precisely, and neither could he.

We had made our way to Court 3 at the old West Side Tennis Club in Forest Hills, Queens, and were loosening up: stretching our shoulders and wrists, running in place, lunging, bouncing on the balls of our feet. I'd decided to enter the 2013 United States Tennis Association Senior National Grass Court Championships, and the tournament organizers had made a number of the courts available for practice in the days before play would begin.

"Maybe it's the texture of the surface, the grass," I said, mostly just to say something. "Or the faintness of the chalk lines?"

"Or that the grass ends about two inches in front of the baselines," Kirill said.

It was true: There was nothing but worn footpaths of dirt along the back edges of the court.

And, upon closer inspection, the grass—ryegrass—within the service boxes and especially at the very back of the court on both sides looked as though it had been worked over by a bogey golfer trying to improve his chip shot. There were divots everywhere, the result, it turned out, of a summerlong weevil infestation.

Still, the two of us were thrilled. "Crazy," Kirill said, taking phantom swings with his racquet and looking around.

Here we were, an evening at summer's end, a hint of fall in the quickly cooling air, the light crepuscular, the Manhattan skyline visible and set against streaks of violet and orange. And looming in the foreground of that vista, the darkened hulk of the old, horseshoe-shaped Forest Hills Stadium, where the U.S. Opens of my youth had been played, and where the game incorporated what I like to think of as its New York refashionings: set-accelerating tiebreakers, equal prize money for female and male players, raucous nighttime tennis under the lights. The last of those Opens was played in Forest Hills in 1977, ten years before Kirill was born. It was news to him that the Open had been played at the stadium. Most people his age probably knew of it, if they knew of it at all, from its appearance as "Windswept Fields" in Wes Anderson's *The Royal Tenenbaums*—the stadium where tennis prodigy Richie Tenenbaum (Luke Wilson), in Björn-Borg-like headband and Fila polo, has, on court, what can only be called a poignantly hilarious nervous breakdown. (The grass court in the movie is a green carpet, impeccable.)

Kirill was my club pro, my year-round tennis coach, my young friend. He was less than half my age. I was nearing my sixty-first birthday, and we were on a grass court in Forest Hills on a weeknight in September because I was attempting to become a serious amateur tennis player—not that I was sure what that meant, exactly. The best sixty-something tennis player at my club in suburban Westchester? Someone who was going to spend his "encore" years, as they were now called—those empty-nested, downshifted years between midlife and something dreadful—as the athlete he had never really been? Here, at Forest Hills, I'd been accepted into the tournament as an unseeded qualifier, which most anyone who was between sixty and sixty-five and a member of the United States Tennis Association could do, though you wouldn't unless you were pretty good, or a masochist. You would be facing the best men's players sixty to sixty-five in the country. I'd only been playing tennis six years. I was in truth a serious novice. I wasn't in their league. But I wanted to get out here and learn what league I was in.

Kirill was teaching me and coaxing me—for hours on end each week—to get there, wherever *there* wound up being. I had been taking lessons with him almost from the beginning, though had been truly training with him, with tireless (or, anyway, panting) determination, for two years. In the tournament, I would be playing men who had been playing tennis all their lives. Many of them had played on their college teams. Like me, they were in their early sixties, which meant they were aging, and feeling it. But for them, as not for me, aging meant seasoned, wiser, in some ways *better*. I was still, after hundreds and hundreds of hours of grueling drills with Kirill, and countless matches against friends, fellow tennis-club members, and opponents from other clubs, not sure how good I was—good as a sixty-something, that is—and, to be honest, not sure what it was I was after from tennis.

And I had never played a match on grass.

We, Kirill and I, started off that evening in Forest Hills with a little mini-tennis, each of us near the net on either side of it: slow-hitting aimed at seeing the ball into the sweet spot of the racquet head, relaxing the swing, tinkering with spins. Kirill urged me to focus—to watch how the ball, off the deadening grass, was failing to bounce any higher than my bent knees; to notice how the matted blades of grass, or what there were of them, enhanced backspin and sidespin. When we both moved away from the net after a few minutes, he instructed me to position myself an inch or two inside the baseline.

"Your game isn't going to work so well here, Gerry," he said. He was standing at the baseline on his side of the net, and he spoke loud enough for me to hear, which meant loud enough for the players tuning up for the tournament on courts to either side of us. What he was saying, and he was right, was that my usual approach, when I stepped onto the green-gray Har-Tru clay of the club where I played and he coached me, was not going to be effective on this surface. On clay, I liked to camp a foot or two behind the baseline—to give the incoming ball time to descend from its high, clay-court bounce into my favored hips-to-knees strike zone; to give myself more time to react to the incoming ball. I ran well side-to-side and in toward the net and back—speed and quickness were the only real advantages I had over most players my age—so court coverage was never a problem for me.

But staying back doesn't win points on grass. Here, I was going to have to come forward to return balls that weren't going to bounce up much, and keep moving in to get to the net. I was going to have to find ways to end points in a hurry: I wouldn't get enough predictable bounces to rally. I was going to have to serve and volley; "chip and charge" on my service returns, especially on serves to my backhand; and, with my forehand, aim audaciously for the corners early, flatly, and with pace. In sum: Against players who were likely to be better than those I typically played against—better than *me*—I was going to have to play a style of tennis I never played. In a *national* tournament.

Kirill hit a dozen or so short balls to me. I netted most of them.

"Short steps, Gerry," he instructed, patiently. "And you have to get lower and stay lower. Lower, and up on your toes. You're bending your knees but leaning back on your heels, leaning back as the ball approaches—you're not getting your body into the shots at all."

I stretched my arms out and raised my palms to the darkening sky.

He moved in closer to the net and demonstrated what he wanted me to do. He moved like a cat. For the life of me I could not understand how, leaning forward and on the balls of his feet, bent low but perfectly balanced, he managed to get to full speed in a few strides, to pounce. He was an athlete: simple, if not so simple, as that.

"One more thing," Kirill said. I rolled my eyes: It was as if I had already mastered the running-while-crouched stuff. "It's very important, here with this grass, to make sure you stop and set before hitting. Even when you are on the run. You will not be able to predict the bounce the ball is going to take the way you can on a hard court or on clay, even. You are going to have to stop and watch."

There was more: "I'd also shorten your swing. Playing inside the baseline, taking the racquet back all the way takes too much time. Get the racquet ready early, as early as possible, but don't take it too far back. You won't have time. You will be hitting late. And coming forward to get a drop shot, get that racquet extended out in front of you and low. Drop shots are not going to bounce up."

The light was fading fast now, and it was getting hard to see the ball. We hit, or sort of hit, for ten more minutes. I liked the way the grass felt under my feet. Grass was supposed to be slippery, but it didn't feel that way to me. It felt spongy, *forgiving*. I was looking for positives.

When we were finished, I told Kirill I felt good about the footing.

"Yeah," he said. "But I think it's supposed to rain a bit this weekend. On and off." I gave him a look, and he laughed. "Hey," he added, "it'll be slippery for the other, guy, too, right?"

2

It was a thought—being a tennis player—that first came to me when I was months from my fifty-fourth birthday and spending what time I could (a few vacation days) wandering the outer courts at the U.S. Open in Flushing, about five miles north of Forest Hills and, New York being New York, a world away. I had been a tennis fan for much of my life but never played. Could I now? And if I started in my mid-fifties, could I get good—good for my age—by the time I was sixty?

Was this a crisis of late middle age? Was it about my oldest son being ready, as I reached my mid-fifties, to look at colleges, and his brother two years behind, and the weekend afternoons already yawning? Did it have something to do with the fact that, no matter how engaged and satisfied I was with being the editor of the *New York Times Magazine*—with having had the good fortune to have done with my professional life what I wanted to do and more—it was almost all behind me now, decades of editing stretching back to the 1970s and my tenure as editor-in-chief three years from being done? Or—and this was very much on my mind by my late fifties, as my editorship of the *Times Magazine* ended and I began to train seriously with Kirill, and magazines everywhere (especially general interest magazines) seemed to be reeling from the Great Digital Disruption and a world I had inhabited since my twenties looked to be dying off: Did I need someplace or something to belong to? Or—and this was how it was more or less seen by my wife, Barbara, who is nine years younger than me; who had known me for more than twenty years when I first brought up taking tennis lessons; who was training for a marathon when we began going out and now swam Olympian laps on the days she was not sweating through Bikram yoga—was it that I was simply not willing to act my age—not willing, with the onset of "young old age" at sixty, to hover in the anteroom of the aged, to reconcile myself to looming extended monotonies, unpromising everydayness?

One of the few inspiriting aspects of entering your sixties, for me anyway, now that I have arrived there, is that you find yourself growing more comfortable with an understanding that you don't necessarily understand your motivations, and never have—that you don't much know yourself in that way at all.

It doesn't work that way with your body. There's little ambiguity with what's going on *there,* and next to no comfort in knowing. That time around turning sixty makes you aware of bodily aging the way your teenage years make you aware—or at least confront you with—what hormones can do. You see it. You sense it, feel it.

There's my face, creased and sagging, greeting me each morning in the bathroom mirror. When I head downstairs and make coffee and fetch the *Times* from my driveway, I turn sooner than I used to to the obituary pages, where seldom a week passes where I don't read about someone I'd known. I search out behaviors and diseases in obits that I can convince myself, however fleetingly, won't get me. I also look at the faces of the men in the paid memoriams. You die in your eighties and your family submits a photo of you taken in your late fifties or early sixties. There's a certain *settledness* to those faces, a sense that there would be no more becoming. It's who you *were*. They're faces like mine.

My hands are speckled with liver spots and ribbed with raised veins. I have arthritis in most of my finger joints, as my mother had, too, already, in her early sixties. My arches have fallen, and those with flat feet are more prone to injuring their hips and legs when they run. I have osteoarthritis in my left knee, which has led to the creation of bone spurs; the knee detectably aches, always. In my left shoulder, tendonitis has come to stay. I am on close terms with Advil.

Some other things you know about your physical self as you enter your sixties: Your lung capacity is in steady decline, as are the fast-twitch muscle fibers that provide power and explosive speed. Your heart is perhaps only 70 percent as efficient as it was when you were thirty. Your prefrontal cortex—where the concentrating and deciding you do gets done—has been shrinking for forty years. Your sight has been diminishing, your other senses, too, and this, along with a gradually receding ability to integrate information you are absorbing and to then issue motor commands, means your balance is not what it used to be, especially under pressure and on the move—which is pretty much how tennis is played.

The good news—for me—was that there was good news, of a sort. Much remains unknown about how aging affects the neural basis of cognition, but what recent studies based on neuroimaging and other techniques have tended to find is that real cognitive slowing is something to start worrying about in your *late* sixties. I *could* still learn (maybe). Moreover, the learning itself was going to be good for my brain, force it to grow: I would, according to the neuroscientists, create new gray matter and synapses. And while empirical data is as yet pretty scarce, there is research that suggests that taking up a new pursuit late in life correlates with better sleep, better immune function, and lower levels of cortisol, the release of which rises in response to stress. The physical and cardiovascular demands of tennis were going to be good for my brain, too, and for the rest of my body. I might live five or six years longer—though there is some research that shows that *really* playing, playing hard, which was my goal, is less likely to lengthen life (because of the strain? The risk of injury?) than taking long walks.

But, really, how much *could* I learn, as I got serious about my tennis in my late fifties? Quite a lot, according to the neuroscientist Gary Marcus. Marcus challenges the neuroscientific consensus that to truly know anything, from a language to a sport, you had to begin as a child. Brain researchers refer to this as the "critical-period effect," and their evidence is based in large part on a study of young barn owls that could—as older barn owls could not—rather easily adapt to what amounted to a virtual-reality experiment in which a prism distorted their perception of things. But then a Stanford neuroscientist, Brian Knutson, found that old owls actually could adapt during this experiment, if you slowed it down and broke up their reorientation to a new environment into smaller parts. Marcus was so buoyed by Knutson's findings that he did an experiment on himself: He learned to play the guitar and wrote an entertaining book about it, *Guitar Zero*. He was forty, not in late middle age, and guitar playing, even, say, in a death-metal band, is not as taxing as tennis playing. Still, I was buoyed by the approach to late learning Marcus posited: Proceed with patience and good humor, tackle the new thing you're doing bit by bit, keep expectations low and persistence high.

3

The halls of the old mock-Tudor clubhouse at Forest Hills that led to the locker room where Kirill and I would shower after practicing were lined with framed photos of the tennis greats who had played in the U.S. Opens held at the stadium. I lingered over them, faded black-and-white action photos of young men in sweaters and long pants and canvas sneakers, elegant young men captured extending themselves with small, wooden racquets. Bill Tilden. René Lacoste. Fred Perry. Bobby Riggs. Jack Kramer. Pancho Gonzales. Rod Laver, that left forearm of his so huge.

I'd begun watching tennis on TV, along with many other Americans, in the mid-1970s. I had never played. I was born in Paterson, New Jersey, and grew up among the sons of truckers and construction workers and factory hands, and no one I knew took tennis lessons, and clubs were places where old men played cards and drank little cups of espresso. I'd hit tennis balls a few times with my college roommate, Ben, who was a real player with a Wilson T2000 and a topspin-generating forehand. He would patiently lob balls across the net to me every once in a while, balls I would return with a borrowed racquet; balls I would return, or try to, as if I were hitting

a shuttlecock. Tennis would be something I would follow—
something engaging and often marvelous at a broadcast distance.

I saw a professional tennis match live for the first time in
the summer of 1982. I was twenty-nine and at loose ends. The
alternative newspaper I'd been working for in New York, the
SoHo News, had folded; I'd been handed a modest severance
check; and I was spending a month in London, living with my
sister, who had a job in banking there. She'd go off to work and
I would read the sports pages of three or four newspapers, then
take a long walk in Hyde Park before settling in for World Cup
soccer, televised from Spain. There were several days when I
made my way to Lord's, in St. John's Wood, to watch cricket:
England v. India. I knew absolutely nothing about cricket,
though I learned fast: Cricket is *intoxicating.*

Sports, watching them and reading about them, has, for
me, always been a consolation. When people ask me what
my favorite childhood memories are, I always bring up my
two summer weeks each year at the Jersey Shore, but seldom
mention that the first thing that always comes to mind is the
New York football Giants—watching games on bleak Sunday
afternoons on our big, consoled, black-and-white TV; or reading about those games in the *Daily News* on Mondays through
the fall; or listening to Marty Glickman's maddeningly detailed
radio play-by-play in the backseat of the car on the way to
one or another aunt's house for Sunday dinner, where the TV
would be tuned not to football but to badly dubbed Italian
biblical films; or going once a year or so to Yankee Stadium
with my father and my uncles to see the Giants from terrible
seats and hear shouts about how Y. A. Title should have thrown
to the *mulignan,* the eggplant, the black; or, on two or three
occasions, when crucial home games were blacked out, driv-

ing north toward Albany with my dad, past motels where you could pay a few bucks to watch the game in a room among strangers—driving to a bar where he would hoist me on his shoulders (I was that young) and I would join the others, the grown and agonizing men, our eyes affixed to a snowy screen above the bar, where the Giants, more often than not, were in the midst of an excruciating game.

It was my sister, through her bank, who secured for me the ticket to Wimbledon. I was thrilled. I borrowed my (then) brother-in-law's blue blazer (several sizes too large) so that I could pop into the bank's on-grounds sponsor's tent and drink a glass or two of champagne.

When you look back and try to assemble a narrative of how you got to some place in your life, and are old enough to understand that you have done this so many times before—that, having lived more than sixty years, there have been so many drafts and rewrites of these narratives, so many hours spent revising the revisions, so much cobbling and retooling and smoothing along the inner contours of your self—you accept, or should, that there will be things misremembered, overlooked, distorted. I can write of my memories, or try to. Neuroscience tells us now that some of those memories will simply be false—that we are wired for creating those. There is also a brain-science theory that every time we summon a memory, we edit or polish it (whether we speak of it or not) and return it to the memory bank changed. Recall something a dozen times, or a hundred times over the course of your life: What resemblance, if any, does it bear to the initial experience? And then there are the things that never get summoned. What of my repressions and forgettings, which, of course, are meaningful, too?

I hold on to an image of no sooner entering the Wimbledon grounds, the morning faintly overcast, than seeing Vitas Gerulaitis heading to a practice court. I know I watched John McEnroe and Peter Fleming (on Centre Court? Or Court No. 1?) win a doubles match that day, and seem to remember McEnroe demanding (could this possibly be true?) that the chair umpire ask a British officer in the stands to remove his peaked cap, the patent-leather visor of which was reflecting the sun that had broken through and, McEnroe loudly groused, was distracting him. Mostly, though, I retain a sense of being by myself all day at the tournament but not lonely. I didn't have a conversation with anyone. And, in fact, it *was* one of the loneliest periods of my life. But there was something about the hushed attentiveness of the spectators; and the players, men and women not much younger than me, mostly, arrayed along the outer courts across the net from one another with no teammates to urge them on or pick them up; and the playing, solitary and exactingly fierce, but beautiful in its near noiseless articulation of form and timeless ritual—there was something in all this, something just this side of revelatory, that unveiled for me a distinction, luminescent and, it turned out, lasting, between loneliness and solitude. Was it some heightened solitude—some more physical manifestation of the thoughtful, careful, solitudinous reading I loved and had devoted my professional life to—that I was after now, in taking up tennis so late in life?

4

Kirill and I, having finished up showering and dressing in the cramped, dank locker room (Rod Laver changed here?!?), had a drink on the club's veranda, the lighted sky-scrapers of the midtown skyline our bar mural. We talked, as we usually talked, about tennis—about Rafael Nadal's impressive, four-set defeat of Novak Djokovic in the final of the recently completed U.S. Open in Flushing (Nadal was having a career year, and Djokovic had endured a grueling semi); about how I would need to "stay strong" (one of Kirill's favorite terms) and not get down on myself against the fine and seasoned players I would face in the tournament. I loved these conversations. A man in his sixties, I liked being coached, coached by a man more than thirty years younger than me.

Kirill Azovtsev, when I first met him, was still in college, twenty years old, only a few years older than my oldest son. He was an assistant pro at the New York Athletic Club's ten-nis facility, on Travers Island in Westchester, not far from the Bronx border in the town of Pelham, where I live. We'd met in a group clinic he led there, and soon after I arranged for a private lesson. I had taken private lessons off and on with one teaching pro, then another, but I could quickly tell that neither wanted to push me, challenge me—take me seriously. They wanted me to have fun during the lessons, but I knew (or was betting I knew) that I would never really enjoy playing until I got good at it. Kirill was different, or so I thought immediately when we stood around and gulped water after that first lesson. He was a little taller than me, broad-shouldered and trim, darkly handsome like the young men in Turgenev's short novels. I asked him about himself, and he told me he'd begun playing tennis when he was eight in St. Petersburg, where he was born. He was an only child, his family comfortable enough, by post–Soviet Russia standards, but not well off. His father, a state-employed customs administrator, wanted him to have a sport. It began with kickboxing.

"It was my father's idea," he told me, "and the first class, Gerry, this kid kicked me in the head."

He still seemed offended.

He'd knocked the boy unconscious.

I tried to register neither surprise nor dismay. "So tennis, then," I said.

"My mother thought it might be a better idea."

The game came easily to him. He played indoors on slick tile courts during the long Russian winters. He preferred serve-and-volley tennis, idolized Pete Sampras and, later, Roger Federer, and began playing competitively as a preteen. As he explained it to me then, there would not have been the money for him to embark on an attempt to be a touring professional—the flights to junior tournaments, the cost of training, eventually, in Spain or Florida—even if he had been good enough. He'd come to America on a tennis scholarship, playing for Concordia College in Bronxville, a few miles north of Pelham. There he'd been part of a team that reached the

Division II top ten. Even before he'd graduated, he'd received training to eventually become a certified tennis instructor.

There was a grace to the way he moved on the court, and a sereneness that belied his youth and had a way of softening—nearly masking, in a teaching setting—a steely competitiveness. You do not get to play top-level college tennis without a felt need to win, or a hatred, or fear, of losing. But those are qualities that do not necessarily make someone a good teacher, and, it's not hard to imagine, could get in the way of teaching—teaching a beginner, a senior beginner like me, anyway. There are so many aspects of what we call temperament, and even now, years later, I am not sure what informs Kirill's on-court calm, his way of seeming at rest within his run. A part of it is that he is simply a great player, someone who can stay on the court and even defeat players ranked in the top five hundred in the world, as he has done. A part of it, too, I have to think, is his respect for and love of the game. Rarely have I spent an hour or two with him when he hasn't said something to me that reflects he's still puzzling out tennis's challenges and frustrations.

One of the things he said to me after that first lesson was this, delivered across the net in his faintly accented, fluent English: "To hit a tennis ball well, so many things have to go right. And then you have to be ready because it is coming right back at you, and you have to do it again."

I knew then I had found my pro: a Russian philosopher.

5

We rode the R train back to Manhattan and settled in for dinner in the saloon at the Oyster Bar restaurant in Grand Central Station, convenient for us both to get our respective trains back to suburban Westchester. (Kirill had an apartment not far from Pelham, but spent a lot of time at his girlfriend's place farther north in White Plains.) The wood-paneled walls of the saloon, the sailing-themed paintings and photographs, and the long oak bar that dominated the room imbued the place with an old-school masculinity. Maybe that's why, after we split a dozen Malpeques and quickly drank better than half our bottle of Sancerre, I found myself wondering aloud to Kirill about competition. I wasn't sure if I truly enjoyed it, I told him. I loved tennis, loved learning. But did I really love going at it with an opponent? And maybe, I suggested, I wasn't sure because I didn't know if competition, for me on a tennis court, was more about winning—relishing that—or about not wanting to lose: fearing that.

"It's different for different people, different players," Kirill said. "And there are differences even within a person. I think for me, I really love winning a point big, when you win it with an ace, or an overhead smash, or a winner down the line. I love going for the winner, and, when you nail it, seeing what it does to the other guy."

I saw him now, at our club, the AC on Travers Island, settling under a high but desperately shallow lob and smashing a winner so hard the ball caromed off the court and over the back fence. I saw the first pump he made after, to himself, mostly.

That had occurred during an afternoon the previous summer. I got to half watch him compete a couple of courts away from where I was playing. Marty, the club's head pro, had arranged for Kirill and another young instructor (and onetime Division II college player) to play a set against two teenagers from the town's high-school tennis team who had recently won the state doubles championship. They were terrific young tennis players—one was headed to play for Marshall, the other to play for Columbia—and Kirill, as a coach and former college player, had played a significant role in their development.

Dozens of club members had gathered on the veranda of the tennis house to watch the set. What intrigued me, as I glimpsed Kirill playing during changeovers in my match, was how he was going to deal with what I saw as a situation fraught with social complication and club etiquette: How do you compete against players you had taught? Players whose parents had paid you for lessons? Would he, Kirill, be nervous? Restrained?

He would not. He and his partner won, 6–1. And from what I saw of it, it was worse than the score indicated.

When I'd met Kirill the next day for a lesson, I'd brought up my concerns. He'd looked genuinely puzzled. "When a match is on, I play to win, period," he'd told me.

Now, at dinner at the Oyster Bar, I asked him how important winning was to him.

"It is *not losing* that is important to me, Gerry." He laughed, took a sip of wine, and leaned forward. "I hate to lose. *Hate it.* Back in Russia, when I was first playing in tournaments: If I lost?" Another sip. "If I lost, I would scream, cry, feel it after for hours, days."

I'd never felt that way as a kid. And I couldn't imagine feeling that way now. Of course, Kirill is a tennis player, in his very being, even if now he only occasionally plays competitively. He spends his weekdays working in Manhattan in commercial real estate and coaches evenings and weekends, leaving little time for him to play matches of his own. If, when he and I are playing, I somehow manage to hit that rare ball that forces him to hit a bad shot, or, even more rarely, get one past him for a winner, I know that during the next rally he is going to forget he is my instructor and crush the ball, hit a winner I never get remotely close to, then quietly say "sorry," as if he were working a little something out.

There's something primal about sports competition, urges and reactions tied up with threat, weakness, potency, domination—sensations seldom registered by someone in his sixties who spent his life editing prose for magazines. Even being the editor of a magazine was not about those things. There is competition there, too, as there is in all realms of human endeavor. But I never felt particularly competitive—envious, deflated, defeated—when another magazine ra[n a] story I admired and wished I had published. (It's dif[ferent] for newspeople, who compete *on* and *for* stories and [to get] scoops first.) Often enough, I dropped a congratul[atory note] to the magazine's editor or directly to the writer. [Wan]ting [to] publish the best reporting, the best thinking, the [best] If any-could. But I didn't feel I was competing *against* [a] [long]-form thing, I thought I was competing *for* somet[hing.]

journalism—that a digitally quickened culture might find it no longer had time for.

"In tennis, I think I compete mostly with myself," I said to Kirill. "If I am playing poorly, I get down on myself. If I am playing well and lose, then the other guy was just better."

Kirill shrugged. "Or just better that day."

I nodded slowly. "Like the guy who beat you in Florida."

This had been months before. One wintry morning after a lesson indoors, Kirill had told me he would not be available the third weekend in March. He would be playing in a tournament in Palm Beach, a national clay-court championship put on by the United States Professional Tennis Association, the association of tennis-teaching pros. He was entering the main event, the men's open singles. It turned out that Barbara was going to be away that weekend in New Orleans, giving a lecture at Tulane—she's an art historian—so I brought up the idea with Kirill of escaping the end of winter and coming to watch him compete. He loved the idea. His girlfriend, Sandy, would be coming, too. She was a club player like me, and we could hit on one of the side courts and hang out while Kirill went through the waiting and warming up that comes with tournament play.

I flew down to Florida on a Friday, after work, and didn't get to the motel where we all were staying till almost eleven. Kirill was asleep by then. He'd texted me that he'd won his first-round match that afternoon, 6–0, 6–2; his second-round match was scheduled for ten the next morning. "Big win! So he'd written.

The tournament was being held in Palm Beach Gardens at a sprawling luxury development called BallenIsles. It's perhaps best known for its golf courses, though a lot of tennis gets played there, too. The Williams sisters have, or have had, mansions there. The tennis-house and sports complex is the size of the White House, with a veranda overlooking the two dozen or so courts, most of them Har-Tru.

The three of us drove out to BallenIsles together that Saturday morning in my rental car, our windows down to take in the warm air that grew faintly salt-scented as we headed east, toward the ocean. It was a lovely morning, with big, passing clouds offering just enough relief from the sun, and Kirill seemed relaxed and not at all preoccupied with his pending match. I wrote in my notebook when we arrived and parked: "He has emotional muscles I will never develop either."

Kirill's match was on the main court, a little stadium that backed onto a parking lot bordered with dwarf palms. There were cement bleachers for five hundred or so and a scoreboard that wouldn't be in use today. There was no chair umpire, and no one watching but Sandy and me. And, it would turn out, we didn't get to watch for long.

Kirill's opponent, Paulo Barros, was older than he was, in his mid-thirties. He coached in Winter Gardens, near Orlando. He was Brazilian, and, watching him warm up, I saw immediately that he played a Latin-style game suitable for the Har-Tru clay—a Western-grip forehand, with huge helpings of topspin; a high-bouncing kick serve; and short-step quickness to the ball. Back in the late '90s he had cracked the top three hundred on the pro tour. He was the top seed here in the men's open singles; he had drawn a bye and not played the day before. He looked more than ready.

Kirill had his serve broken in the first set. Barros easily held his, hitting his topspin forehands deep, driving Kirill back, from where he hit returns that came up short and opened up angles for Barros, who was finding the lines for easy winners. Kirill was broken again in the third game, double-faulting twice. He would continue having trouble with his serve. He tried playing serve-and-volley, but Barros passed him more times than not. It would all be over in forty minutes or so, with Kirill never winning a game: 0–6, 0–6.

I found it painful to watch—it had reminded me of nothing so much as watching my younger son, Luca, pitching for his traveling baseball team as a twelve-year-old and suddenly and irredeemably losing the strike zone. Luca would get so angry with himself, despairing, inconsolable. But Kirill was not suffering after his loss. "Come on, he was painting the lines from the beginning, he was just on," he had told me afterward. Barros had not been *essentially* better but *situationally* better. That Barros went on to win the tournament handily did not change Kirill's assessment. What Kirill was experiencing was something psychologists call "self-serving bias." Athletes use this to protect their egos and cope with loss: I win, I'm better; I lose, you had a good or lucky day. Psychologists also are not surprised that those who hate to lose are drawn to sports: Losing within the confines of a game, the thinking goes, is actually a way of controlling and limiting that pain that accompanies loss.

I asked Kirill—we were finishing up our dinner and working our way through a second bottle of wine, the Oyster Bar emptying—to talk more about losing. How, as someone who hates to lose, had he gone from being such an emotional loser to one who took losing in stride? He credited his father. His father, he said, was at his side whenever he played as a youth. They traveled together to matches. When Kirill needed better coaching, his father found it. His father stood up for him. His father told him that on the court, he needed to be "a lone warrior, always." His father taught him the proper way to act on a court, win or lose, and he internalized that.

"My father," he said, "he was my best friend. He was always there for me. My mother came to think my tennis was a waste of money, but not my father. He worked nights so he could be at every match, every practice."

"You miss him."

"I do."

"You think of going back to Russia?"

"Never. I'll never go back."

He then began a long and complicated story about his father, about how he had a good job in customs in St. Petersburg, and then was asked to step aside by higher-ups so that they could put "their man," as Kirill put it, in the post. Kirill's father refused. "Next thing you know," Kirill said, speaking more slowly now, "he's set up. Like he did something corrupt, it's made to look like. And then he's taken away. And though he is able to prove he's innocent in the end, he spends a year and a half away. I was thirteen. It just blew up everything. Every day, I would come home after school and find my mother and grandmother crying."

Kirill looked like he was about to cry. He told me he didn't like to talk about this. But he kept talking. "The plan from then on was to get me out of Russia—that tennis could maybe earn me a scholarship to come to the United States. My father and I took an overnight train to Moscow so I could try a third time to pass the SAT and be NCAA eligible. I had coffee for the first time. And I passed by a point. And Concordia College offered me this deal where they would cover sixty percent of the costs, and I would do work-study for the rest."

He took a deep breath and took a big gulp of wine. He said that someday he'd like to bring his mother and father here, to the States, but there was his grandmother who needed to be cared for, and that, anyway, "leaving is not easy for any person." He then said—changing the subject, or not—that he'd like to learn to box someday, and went into a story about how back in St. Petersburg, when he was thirteen, that time seemingly so palpable to him now, as we drank, he'd been punched in the face by a youth outside an ice-cream parlor as he, Kirill, tried to protect his cousin's new bicycle from being stolen.

I paid the check. We embraced and got our trains. I thought, during much of my ride home, that real athletes, at such a young age, are often playing for stakes—psychological, or economic, or, in Kirill's case, what amounted to political—that someone like me will never fully apprehend. Tennis, winning at it, sent him on his way, and also steeled and buttressed his inner life, gave him that Emersonian self-reliance of his. I recalled how he told me once: "In tennis, it is just you, and I always liked that. No excuses. I feel good in that situation."

That is his situation. He counts on himself now. So much else is so far away.

6

The following morning I got up and e-mailed Alexandra, who I'd been regularly e-mailing for many months now. Alexandra Guhde, under the name Arienna Lee, was a tennis blogger. She blogged under an alias because she was also a serious Bay Area Jungian psychotherapist, and wanted to keep those identities separate, though any avid reader of the blog—and I was very much one—could see she had failed at that. The blog was called *Extreme Western Grip,* named for the way her favorite on-court analysand, Rafael Nadal, holds his racquet when hitting his big topspin forehand and, perhaps, for her own powerfully loopy left-coast perspective. She blogged about professional tennis matches, watching most of them on TV in her Berkeley apartment, but also managed to work in riffs about Greek mythology, Jane Austen, pop culture, and psychological theory. I'd e-mailed her a mash note about her blog, and we'd struck up an e-mail correspondence. We'd write back and forth about matches we watched, and about our tennis games—she'd played in high school, and was getting back into it after a hiatus. And as we got to know each other, I was increasingly interested to get her thoughts on what she imagined I was up to with tennis.

Jungians, like Jung himself, talk a lot about the "second half of life," a concept most clearly articulated in James Hollis's bestseller *Finding Meaning in the Second Half of Life: How to Finally, Really Grow Up,* the subtitle more than hinting at what he thinks about what you've been up to in the first half of life. I went through a self-help-book phase right around the time I was deciding whether to get serious with Kirill and double the hours I was spending with him—books I would never read in public or discuss with anyone (we all have our vanities), even as I learned that the greatest tennis writer America has ever produced, David Foster Wallace, had been a careful reader and rereader of John Bradshaw, Alice Miller, M. Scott Peck, and others. (He was also a suicidal depressive.) My problem with these books, beyond how jargony and padded they tend to be, is that, to, yes, oversimplify, I wasn't *un*happy with the life I'd lived or the life I then had. Jung thought the second half of life began around age thirty-five, but then the patients he was seeing back then were not likely to live as long as (fingers crossed) I will. It was then, in middle age, that, as Jung saw it, one realized one's life lacked meaning, that one was living the life (marriage, career) others (i.e., the internalized negative mother) had wanted *for* one: that one's soul ached and needed tending.

Now, really, whose soul doesn't need tending to? And—because I am seeing a therapist shaking her head here—yes, there are things down there in the unconscious, home to shadowy impulses and unmet longings, that I am not aware of, and maybe I should begin by writing down what I recall of my dreams, writing them down in the dark, as one Jungian (not Alexandra) once advised me at a dinner party, because the light would steal some of it.

Alexandra *did* think there were unconscious forces urging

me to get more serious about my tennis, double my hours with Kirill, play competitively. She didn't know what they were, or continued to be, but she thought that was great: To have a restless unconscious meant there were strong internal stirrings at work that I allowed to "go about their business," as she put it over dinner in Oakland the first time we met in person. (I was in the Bay Area to attend my oldest son's college graduation, and that was accompanied by *lots* of internal stirrings . . .) She also told me, and it rang so true for me, which may be another way of saying it confirmed what I had been thinking but was unable to articulate all along: "Personally," she said, "I don't see any reason why someone who is satisfied cannot also be *un*satisfied—insomuch as *still seeking*." It was like when I read somewhere that you could be both a happy person and an unhappy person, because happiness and unhappiness, according to what neuroscience had discovered, were situated in and triggered by different sides of the brain—were discrete and did not cancel each other out. Some people were very happy and very unhappy, too. Me, I was a sunny melancholic. Now I could see I was a satisfied seeker.

"The whole point is the *search* for meaning," Alexandra said to me with real conviction. "And there are lots of different meanings to be found in life."

There were. I wanted, for instance, to see what meanings I could tease from my aging body. There's a passage from Cyril Connolly in his epigrammatic meditation, *The Unquiet Grave*—a book I love—in which he writes, "The supreme liberty is liberty from the body." Is he (following centuries of classical and Christian thinking, by the way) *out of his mind*? I had, like him, spent most of my life reading, editing, looking for meaning in prose. But I wanted a new kind of attentiveness, and I wanted to move, to get somewhere as quickly as

I could—to a tennis ball, say. I wanted to understand how my muscles worked, and I wanted to strengthen them. I also wanted to command those muscles and that movement, through the learning of proper form and technique: I wanted to enter a structure, a discipline, and come to do something the right way, which also happens to be beautiful.

Could I overcome what the philosopher and former dancer Maxine Sheets-Johnstone has called "cephalocentricity"—the life of the mind with all its inwroughtness, its resonances and satisfactions tucked down inside oneself—and come to know things I didn't through body movement? Could I slow the mind to the matters at hand, achieve that *presentness* sport holds the promise of, achieve what another philosopher (and tennis player), Colin McGinn, has described as the pleasant existential aloneness a sports activity can provide, a certain "muscular solipsism"? (Okay, I cannot *not* seek meaning in prose.) Is there, in the end, an examined *physical* life?

Obviously, to play tennis well, more than the body is involved. There is strategy and judgment. I would need to acquire skills, and that would require practice—which would require self-motivation. And the skills involved in learning to play tennis would require precise perceptual mastery (is that ball headed toward me across the net loaded with topspin or backspin?) and exacting coordination among multiple muscles (begin moving in and get lower to take that ball-deadening backspin shot). The muscle that is my brain would have to grow in new ways.

I wanted to do something *difficult.* Maybe that was, in the end, why I wanted to try to play tennis.

I did have a longing to get better at something—I was aware of *that. Improving* was such a small part of my life now. I had been a very good reader since I was a small child. I went on to essentially read for a living. I had probably stopped improving as a reader half a life ago. We stop getting better at things, tangible things, so early on.

Finally, I wanted, one last time, perhaps, to struggle at something I could control, because the last real struggles were going to be ones I could not. I wanted to push my body to its limits before it pushed me to mine. I had a hunch that testing yourself might be the ultimate means to freedom, *felt* freedom. I was going to train for years, and make as much time for that as I could—which would never be enough: Tennis, I believed, is the most difficult sport there is to master, requiring speed *and* endurance *and* hand-eye coordination *and* psychological toughness.

It was my psychological toughness I was worrying about when I e-mailed Alexandra this particular morning. I was taking the day off, but I was anything but relaxed. I was going to be meeting and hitting later that morning with a senior-tennis legend of sorts, and was beyond anxious.

Bob Litwin is one of the best senior amateur tennis players America's ever had. The United States Tennis Association begins considering you a "senior" when you are in your thirties, and organizes regional and national tournaments around the country for men and women at which participants are grouped, according to their age, at intervals of five years: forty and over, forty-five and over, up through age ninety (God bless them). Litwin played in a few eastern regional tournaments before entering his first USTA national championship, the Men's 35 National Clay Championships, where he lost in a hurry. He kept entering national tournaments and eventually, in 1990, won the National Grass Court Championships for men thirty-five to forty. He was forty-one. (The USTA permits you to play "younger.") He has kept winning. He has garnered, at last count, seventeen USTA national titles and countless regional ones. (There was an eleven-year stretch of eastern-regional play during which Litwin never lost a match.) He has been a member of many U.S. senior Davis Cup teams, and, in 2005, in Perth, Australia, won the International Tennis Federation's Men's 55 World Championships—yes, senior tennis is a global phenomenon. Litwin that year became the world's No. 1–ranked tennis player in his age group, and has continued to compete at the highest levels nationally and internationally as he's gotten to that stage of life—he had just turned sixty-five—where he is considered a senior by the Social Security Administration. A colleague of mine knew Litwin through one aspect of his day job—as a performance coach for Wall Street traders and hedge-fund analysts—and he arranged for us to talk, and also to hit for an hour at the club Litwin belonged to, Shelter Rock, in Manhasset on the North Shore of Long Island, a half hour from my place in Westchester.

I was anxious, I knew, or thought I knew, because I was afraid of embarrassing myself on the court with Litwin, and uncomfortable with the envy I worried I'd feel when I saw how much better a player he was than me.

I wrote Alexandra and told her this, or something like this.

She was, as usual, reassuring, sort of. "Why shouldn't you delight in sharing the court with a man who has finely honed skills?" she wrote back. "You know what it takes to get good at something, you are in the middle of that process yourself now."

I wrote back and told her I didn't like being envious. It was wrong, which for me meant guilt on top of the envy, and also alien.

Alexandra responded: "I heard an interview recently with Linda Ronstadt on *Fresh Air*"—the public-radio show. "She was talking about the first time she heard Emmylou Harris sing. She, Ronstadt, said something like, 'Her voice was incredible, and I could either stand to the side and envy her, or try to meet her and sing with her.' I really liked that way of putting it. Envy is an initial recognition of a capacity. Nothing wrong with recognizing."

She added: "Of course, getting beyond the initial recognition is something not everyone does."

You see what I mean about "reassuring, sort of."

7

I was still anxious as I made my way in slow traffic over the Throgs Neck Bridge, despite having corresponded with Alexandra, stretched for twenty minutes, and then hit for longer than that against the wall at my club.

Shelter Rock had a '60s-modern feel, the clubhouse low-slung with lots of glass, the more than two dozen Har-Tru courts hidden by hedgerows that could not diminish the traffic din from the Long Island Expressway. I sat in a leather chair in the club lobby, near an imposing stone fireplace, waiting, as arranged, for Litwin, and watching men and women older than me ambling and shuffling by in foursomes: retirees with the time to have standing doubles matches late on a weekday morning.

Litwin, approaching me, was taller than I had imagined, which is to say taller than five-foot, ten-inch me, and when he extended his hand (a racquet tucked under his right arm) and said hello, his voice was almost gentle—which is not what I thought you sounded like when you'd spent your life competing and winning. There was a youthfulness to his look—a boyish smile, and hair that, combed back, curled behind his ears and nearly reached the base of his neck. His tennis shirt and shorts were the limited-edition, lichen-green ones Uniqlo had designed for Novak Djokovic to wear earlier that summer at the French Open (this is the kind of stuff you notice as a tennis fan), and when I mentioned this to Litwin, he related how he'd played doubles once with Djokovic, at a party thrown by one of his Wall Street clients—a backyard party, where the backyard included a private tennis court, and the guest list featured one of the very best players in the world, racquet at the ready.

"He was really a gentleman, not blown up with himself at all, and smart, and funny," Litwin said of Djokovic as we made our way outside. "He immediately got the level of players we were and played down to it. He was terrific with my client's son, offering tips on technique. But what most impressed me was how much he enjoyed playing, even these few games of doubles with players like me.

"It sounds so simple, but that is key," Litwin went on to say. "Are you enjoying yourself when you are playing? And if not, why not?"

We stopped and stood on a patio that overlooked rows of courts, not many of them empty. "This club was built in an era when some of the tennis clubs and country clubs here on Long Island were still restricted," Litwin said evenly. "No Jews allowed. So here was a new club where Jews could be members."

I'd read of how Litwin had played and coached at the World Maccabiah Games, the so-called Jewish Olympics, held every four years in Israel. And, in 2004, at a fifty-five-and-over USTA senior championship tournament in Philadelphia, he had forfeited the finals rather than play on Yom Kippur.

I told him there were no tennis clubs where I was born, in Paterson—or, anyway, none that I knew of.

"I grew up in Great Neck"—just east of Manhasset—"and learned to play on public courts," he said, scanning the Shelter

Rock courts for one we could play on. "My father would play with his friends and I would watch—that was my first exposure to tennis. But you go back to the twenties here and along the Gold Coast"—he meant the towns on Long Island Sound: Kings Point, Sands Point . . . Gatsby's Long Island—"you had tennis pros living on the estates of these wealthy men."

Bob excused himself for a moment, and walked at a quick pace toward a man I assumed controlled who had which court when. I noticed, as he moved, a slight, side-to-side rocking motion in his gait—not a limp, exactly, but something. When he came back, a court secured for an hour, I asked him if he was feeling all right, physically.

"Two hip surgeries—one, then another," he told me. "It's taken a couple of years to get back to form, but I think I am there now, feeling good, and thankful for that."

We played a little mini-tennis, then moved back to the baselines. The clay was sandy, slippery, and, not having my footing yet, I kept the ball toward the middle of the court, or tried to, and Bob did the same. The first thing I noticed was that he was not going to drive me back from the baseline with his power, the way Kirill can. It struck me then that there were not going to be many men in their sixties—men my age—who could. *Comforting.* No sooner had I had this thought, though, than it was displaced by two other observations: Bob was completely relaxed. And Bob was not missing any ball that he got to. He flowed with confidence and consistency. When play stopped because neither of us had a ball in our pocket to put in play, all the balls were hugging the bottom of the net on *my* side. *Deflating.*

We picked up the tempo, began varying our shots, going for the lines, moving each other around. Litwin was a lefty, like me, and, like me, he looked for opportunities for his sharply angled crosscourt forehands and mostly sliced his backhand to stay in points. I tried several times to run around my backhand and hit an inside-out forehand to his backhand, in the corner. When I hit one past him for a winner, he stopped and said: "That's a good shot. But you've made only one of the five of those you've tried. Is that something you want to use in a match?"

A few minutes later, I came to net on one of his backhand slices, had a routine forehand volley, and dumped it in the net. I softly, or maybe not so softly, tapped the net cord with my racquet three times.

Bob approached me.

"Why so negative? You had a good idea, you set up the point really well, and you missed a sitter. You got wristy and wobbly on the volley. So what? You won't miss it next time. Do you think when you play a tennis match that the goal is to not miss a shot?"

This, I quickly understood, was Litwin in performance-coach mode. Surprising myself, I liked it.

"Where is all that negativity coming from, Gerry? Do you know you grimace, just a little, but you grimace every time you miss? Why? You are a sixty-year-old man with the good fortune to be out on a tennis court on a sunny morning. Look at us!"

He turned to the chain-link fence that ran along the side of the court. "I want you to imagine the people who love you are here, watching you, supporting you. Me, I always imagine my father. Others, too. Who are your angels?"

It was a question I hadn't asked myself. Ever. Which is not to say I shouldn't have. A picture came to mind of a young nun I'd had in a catechism class when I was nine or ten. She'd told us we had guardian angels, and afterward, walking home, a classmate of mine, Johnny Di Martino, had told me with the confidence he brought to all things that guardian angels were female and naked.

"I am going to stop play every time I see you grimace or drop your head," Bob said, bringing me out of my reverie. "You have got to get your mind right. It's at the core. Otherwise, you will not play well when it matters."

We backed up to the baselines and began hitting again. I did try to stop grimacing, mostly by laughing as I found myself grimacing. Bob served—a tough, lefty spin serve—and I returned. I served (less tough) and he returned. My mind was, or so I thought, where it tends to be when I am on a tennis court: in a better place than most anywhere else.

Bob approached the net; our hour was up. We shook hands the way tennis players do.

"You have a nice game, Gerry," he said. "The crosscourt forehand, the slice backhand when you keep it low. If it were a match, I would win three of every five points." It was as painless a way as I could imagine to convey that I'd be beaten down, shutout, double bageled in a best-of-three-set match against him.

We walked to the club restaurant, got a table, and ordered lunch. Bob filled in some of his story: He'd played tennis at Great Neck South High School, tried out for the team at the University of Michigan but didn't make it, then put his racquet away. He'd gotten a teaching job in the early '70s at a private school in Manhattan, been made the tennis coach, liked it, and gone on to coach tennis at clubs on Long Island. He developed a series of Zen-like self-affirmation techniques he called "The Focused Game" that he began teaching in the late '70s and eventually turned into a business. He'd married his high-school sweetheart, divorced, remarried, and, twenty-six years later, lost his second wife to cancer—"the toughest thing," he told me, as if it were months ago, and not three years; he'd recently married again. He'd injured his hip during a sixty-and-over tournament in Florida, chasing a ball and flipping over a low wall. He'd had one surgery to replace the hip, then another to fix the surgery. This had sidelined him for a couple of years, but now he was back to playing. He was preparing for the USTA's Men's 65 National Grass Court Championships, to be held at a club on the Jersey Shore. (He would win both the singles and doubles.)

I mentioned that I would be playing in the sixty-and-over grass-court championships at Forest Hills.

"Good," he said, immediately, enthusiastically, but nothing more.

Lunch arrived, an omelet for Bob, a turkey club for me. I was famished, as I always am, post-tennis, and he was, too.

"Who plays in these tournaments?" I asked after wolfing down half the sandwich in silence.

"Lot of the regulars in their sixties are coaches or former coaches." Then, reading my mind, he added: "You might win a first-round match. You move well. After that, unless you run into someone making an inordinate number of mistakes . . ."

He leaned in. "Let me ask you, Why are you doing this?"

"Why am I entering the tournament?"

"No, playing tennis, taking up tennis at this point. Why? Why now? What are you in this for?"

I told him about how much I'd been enjoying the process of getting better, learning new shots, the practicing—having a practice, in that way. I liked the aloneness of singles tennis, I said. I ventured that tennis coaxed me out of my intimations of mortality for an hour or so, and watched for his reaction.

"That's good. And it's keeping you in shape. You're in the kind of shape a lot of people your age are not, or can't be."

It was true. I was training with Kirill for hours each weekend, and playing matches for hours more. And for two years I'd been hitting the gym most weekday mornings before work. I'd gleaned from blogs and websites what top tennis players were doing in their workouts and cobbled together my own routine. I did thirty minutes of interval training twice a week on a stationary bike, sprinting up imaginary hills and, eventually, sweating and gasping and getting my heart rate to the 80 percent maximum of a forty-year-old. I did stations at weight machines. I dabbled in plyometrics, a favorite now among elite players: These are exercises that involve a lot of jumping, and are said to improve balance and explosive power. I did yoga stretches I picked up from attending classes with my wife, stretched every day for ten or fifteen minutes. I also all but stopped eating red meat and became what my *Times* colleague Mark Bittman calls a flexitarian; I was eating lots of grains and greens and beans and limiting to one meal, lunch or dinner, a serving of chicken, fish, or eggs. The body that I couldn't coax to do what I wanted it to do on a tennis court was the fittest body I'd ever had. My waist was down to the size it had been when I graduated from college—thirty inches—and I was, at 140, a dozen pounds heavier, mostly in my more muscular upper body and thighs. A test I took had put my "biological" age at forty-six. Sometimes, after getting drubbed in a match, I'd remind myself, in a give-thanks way, that most men my age are overweight or obese, and that 20 to 30 percent of them have health conditions that prevent them from working, never mind chasing a drop shot.

"What else?" Bob was asking now. He had a relaxing voice, low and pause-woven, like that of an overnight FM-radio DJ from the late '60s. "Are you becoming a better *person* on the court? Are you drawing on your good story? That's what I was trying to begin to get at with you today."

I wasn't sure what he meant by that, which did not stop me from being intrigued. But there wasn't going to be time to discuss it. His wife arrived. She was younger than he, very pretty in a tennis dress, and was carrying two tennis racquets that turned out to be his. He was off to play elsewhere, and running a little late.

I told him how I would like to talk more about his performance-coaching program, and he said that maybe the best way to learn about it was to enroll in the course.

"It's about getting more of what you really want, becoming more of who you really want to be," he said.

I laughed as I caught myself grimacing. And I knew I would take him up on it.

8

It was a dazzlingly sunny Friday afternoon in late September, and I was back on the veranda of the West Side Tennis Club in Forest Hills for a cocktail reception to welcome the sixty-four players in the sixty-and-over draw. I was to have played my opening-round match that morning, and had planned to take the day off, but won in a walkover, unopposed, my opponent, for some reason, unable to make it to New York from his home in Massachusetts. I'd been on edge all day Thursday about the timing of the match, which wasn't to be announced until Thursday evening. I would have meetings at work to reschedule. This was not an issue for the first clutch of players I introduced myself to at the reception. They commented on my being in a business suit—they were in their tennis whites. I asked how they'd done in their first-round matches. It turned out they were all seeded players who'd earned first-round byes. They'd gotten in a little practice that afternoon. I noticed that at their feet they had racquet bags that held three, four racquets, all with fresh, white grips—like pro players. None of them had a day job, other than giving tennis lessons.

One of them asked what I did, and I explained that I'd been a magazine editor all my life, and had edited the *Times*

Magazine until a couple of years ago, and was now involved in getting the *Times* into new businesses. I went on to say that I had begun playing tennis only six years before, and had really gotten into it only in the past two years. They looked at me the way you look at a guy you've just met whose fly is wide open.

I excused myself and made my way to the bar. It was crowded, and it took some time to get a glass of white wine. I struck up a conversation with a player named Victor Aguilar. He was solidly built, with black hair slicked back '50s style from his receding hairline, his tanned skin set off suavely by his white shorts and polo. He told me he had recently retired as the head coach of the University of Texas at El Paso women's tennis team. He'd been born in El Paso, and been a No. 1–ranked boys' junior player there before moving to Denver to attend high school and play more competitive tennis. In his junior and senior years, in the early 1970s, he won Colorado State singles championships.

"I played a match in Denver at an event where Arthur Ashe was playing the main match," he told me. "He was my hero back then." He raised his beer bottle toward the old, crumbling stadium. "And now I am here, where he won." Ashe won the Open at Forest Hills in 1968—the first of the open era, when professionals were invited to play along with amateurs—in a grueling five-set match against the Dutchman Tom Okker. (Ashe's victory in his semifinal match, against fellow-American Clark Graebner, is immortalized in John McPhee's taut masterpiece of a tennis book, *Levels of the Game*.)

"At that event, in Denver, the strangest thing I remember," Victor was saying now, "I had posed after with Arthur Ashe for a photo, and some kid asked for my autograph. *Mine.* There was Arthur Ashe. And he asked for my autograph. I wonder what he did with it?"

Victor went to Southern Illinois University on a tennis scholarship, then played for Regis College in Denver before finishing up his degree at UTEP. He taught history for a time in an El Paso public school and at a local community college. He played a lot of local senior tennis through his coaching years, and was his city's best. This was his first year on the national seniors circuit. He'd enter a tournament, he said, then book himself a room in a cut-rate motel for one night, booking a next night if he won that day. He kept to himself evenings, eating inexpensively and getting to bed early, though for this tournament, in New York, his wife had joined him. He was playing well, and winning, and was ranked in the top ten for sixty-year-olds.

"This is, for me, the fulfillment of a dream," he said. I think I knew what he meant, even if he was not going to elaborate on that. He was competing again against the best; he was confident he belonged here; he was a brother in a kind of fraternity, despite the fact that he was here to defeat as many of these players as he could and win the championship. He was not battling to *be* here. He was, in a way, back home. "First time I have been playing nationally since my high-school days," he said. "Some of the guys at these tournaments I played against when I was a high-school kid in Denver—can you believe that?"

On the train ride home, I found myself thinking about the work of Stuart Brown, a psychiatrist who has done a good deal of clinical research into the nature of play. Much of that research had figured into a cover story we did on play in the *Times Magazine.* Brown has this idea that each of us—not only athletes like Victor—has a "play history": a personal, emotionally complicated narrative of our childhood experiences of games and sports that we might find useful to shape from our memories later in life.

Brown's outlook was California cloudless: He was working out of a tree-house office in Carmel Valley when the magazine profiled him, and his emphasis, drawn from his study of patients, was on finding the childlike joy we'd experienced in play. But he allowed that playing, like childhood, can mean different things to different people, and he'd constructed a taxonomy of "play personalities" that I found convincing. I am what Brown calls a kinesthete, one of those who "want to push their bodies and feel the result."

I had played sports as a boy, pushing my body, but the result was not always (or even mostly) childlike joy. In every grade-school class photo, I'm in the front row, among the shortest boys. And I was the skinniest, despite periods of drinking something called Instant Breakfast with most meals. I did play baseball, basketball, and football, or attempted to. I was fast, won grade-school trophies for sprinting, but something that was over in a matter of seconds could leave you only so joyful.

Running back a punt in a Police Athletic League football game, running up the sideline twenty, thirty, forty yards, past boys taller and forty pounds heavier than me, hearing nothing but my breathing, an eighty-five-pound thirteen-year-old with this electrifying sense of having the muddied field, the whole November afternoon, to myself, even as hundreds of eyes were on me and only me, I did feel something that I would call ecstatic. Then I was hit helmet to helmet by the punter—I never saw him angling across the field—and knocked unconscious. My mother never let me play football again.

The other things I most vividly remember about playing and competing as a youngster begin with those electrifying flashes—moments of drama or exhilaration that a kid seeks from sports; that his radio and TV and morning sports section have taught him to dream of—only to darken, and remind him of the fear and sense of weakness that is never far from present in a small, skinny, and perhaps too sensitive boy growing up in a place a little tougher than he was. There was a Babe Ruth League baseball game the summer between my seventh- and eighth-grade years, a warm July night in a park on the east side of Paterson near the Passaic River, and in the bottom of the sixth inning (the games were seven innings long) I broke up a no-hitter with a bunt single that also brought home what would be the winning, and only, run from third base—Tony Lombardo, even shorter than me, had walked and stolen two bases. I couldn't hit, not at this level; this was only my third hit in six, seven weeks of playing, and none had left the infield. Suddenly, for the first time (and only time, it would turn out) in my life, I was the hero of a game, which rated a brief mention in the following day's *Paterson Evening News*.

A couple of weeks later, we faced the same team again, on a different field in a different part of town, near a set of postwar housing projects behind my church, St. Gerard's. It was the same pitcher, too, a stocky Puerto Rican kid, and the first time I got up, he threw straight at my head. I dove out of the way, got back in the batter's box, and watched the second pitch sail behind me.

I turned to the home-plate umpire and said, "He's throwing at me."

"Don't bunt to break up a no-hitter," he said without looking at me.

The third pitch struck my left calf, hard, severely bruising my fibula, ending my season and my stint in organized youth baseball.

What I enjoyed playing most was basketball, despite my size. I couldn't and didn't score much, but I was a quick defender and a good passer. What I mostly loved, though, was

47

the constant running, and the feeling, once I was old enough to play in a league, of being inside in a warm gym sweating on cold afternoons and evenings. I played for several years on a P.A.L. team for grade schoolers, and at the end of the winter of my eighth-grade year, in the last game of a dismal season in which we had managed to win only a couple of games, we—the only team of white kids in the league—played the first-place team, who had yet to lose a game. And somehow, in a tiny gym downtown behind Paterson's city hall, a gym encircled above by a wooden running track that made it impossible to shoot from the corners—not that we often would—we *won*! We gathered in front of our bench for the postgame lineup for team handshakes, shouting and clapping and shouting some more—until two or three of the opposing players rushed us and began whaling on us. Our coach, Mr. Hernandez, a former semipro boxer, jumped in to break things up, as did their coach, and I got shoved and knocked back, not punched like some of our better players. But I was scared, and humiliated for being so scared, and bewildered that things could take such an emotional turn. And though I would throughout my life turn that night and that game and its aftermath into a funny story, as I would so many other incidents from my childhood, I knew somewhere inside myself that sports had mostly taught me that moments of excitement and accomplishment are not only fleeting but dangerous somehow, and that if I was feeling joy about something, I would soon enough be seized by dread.

I managed not to be cut from my high-school basketball teams because coaches liked having me around. I listened, remembered instructions and plays, was *coachable*. I almost never got in a game (and these were losing teams I played on). My fondest memories are of practices held between Christmas and New Year's, when there was no school—of having a heated, skylit gym to go to on frigid mornings and spending hours running drills. But my interests were drifting elsewhere, to the school paper and the literary magazine. I was watching sports as much as ever, particularly pro football, especially my and my father's and my uncles' beloved Giants. With money from a busboy job I had at an Italian restaurant, I was also betting on football regularly and pretty heavily, and, for a time, running a weekly football gambling game for a local bookie out of one of the school's boys' rooms. But I wasn't playing much anymore. At college I began running—it was the early '70s, and everybody was running—but that wasn't playing. Nor, later, was the time I spent on a rowing machine in my Upper West Side studio, or riding my ten-speed around and around Central Park, to burn off work anxiety and keep in shape. Later still, I loved the hours and hours I spent tossing baseballs and footballs with my young sons, which was sort of playing, but parenting really isn't about you, or better not be.

And then, so quickly it seemed, the kids were teenagers, and I was borrowing a tennis racquet from my neighbor Steve, who had been a national USTA champion and had two daughters who had played Division I college tennis out west, like Victor. I was starting a new volume of my play history. Or was I trying to rewrite the old one?

9

I didn't sleep all that well the night before my first match at the grass-court nationals. But it had little to do with the match. I wake in the middle of the night all the time now. Sometimes it's my left shoulder, with its tendonitis, objecting to being slept upon. Or a foot might cramp, or a knee may be abrading the other because the pillow meant to keep them apart has slipped away somewhere. Or it could be I just have to pee: Benign prostatic hyperplasia is common to men in their sixties. And once you are awake you will have to pee. Or, anyway, I will.

I rise, blinking and feeling my way in the dark, trying not to wake up Barbara, and seldom do. She could sleep through an air assault (not that I'm envious or anything). I pad down the hall, thinking inevitably, despite efforts not to, of Philip Larkin and his deep-going, dispiriting poems of being awake when you shouldn't be, awake and thinking night thoughts: the 4 a.m. piss in "Sad Steps," with its "reminder of the strength and pain / Of being young; that it can't come again," and, always, some part of his last great poem, "Aubade," in which, up again at four—and not aubade-like; he is *not* sneaking out of his lover's bed—the poet can't dispel thoughts of "The sure extinction that we travel to / And shall be lost in always. Not to be here / Not to be anywhere, / And soon; nothing more terrible, nothing more true." And he was only fifty-five! (Though dead, and soon, at sixty-three.)

In the yellowish glow of the bathroom night-light, half asleep, I see Stan, or anyway the photographs of him— Stanislas Wawrinka, the second-best Swiss tennis player of his generation. (Talk about the pain of being young: He has beaten his friend and countryman Roger Federer exactly three times, in twenty tries.) On a bookshelf above the toilet, I keep propped up and open an old, crinkly copy of *Tennis* magazine with a spread of four time-lapse photos of Wawrinka's drive-backhand swing. Wawrinka has the best one-handed backhand I have ever seen. He also has tattooed on his left forearm the following, from Samuel Beckett's *Worstword Ho*: "Ever tried. Ever failed. No matter. Try again. Fail again. Fail better." Those are words I was living by when I had a racquet in my hand.

I've looked longer and harder at these pictures than at any of my wife or sons. I've scrutinized the weight loaded up on his back foot so he can push into the shot; the front shoulder turned so far that it seems to brush his chin; the straightness of his hitting elbow; and, finally, his non-hitting left arm, as the shot is completed, outstretched to counterbalance, as if he is a tenor, hitting just the right note. Which he is.

Did I mention my backhand drive sucks?

I return to bed and roll onto my non-hitting shoulder and shut my eyes, despite knowing that sleep won't come quickly. The night thoughts, the dreadful equations of aging, seize hold: I've lived longer in the past than I can possibly expect to live in the future; I have more to remember than I have to look forward to. I've never been someone kept awake much by work, except when a reporter was in some dangerous part of Iraq, say, and hadn't been in touch. I did have a problem sleeping as a child, kept awake by what the nuns told me a wrathful god was capable of doing to me, eternally. To take my mind off that I would turn away from the crucifix that hung above my light switch and line up my six or seven stuffed animals next to me, imagining them a football team, with me as their head coach in a cashmere topcoat and fedora, the NFL style of the late '50s. We'd play games against teams of my conjuring. I remember regularly beating the Justice League of America—Batman, the Flash, the Green Lantern, and the rest—and once crushing the cast of *Bonanza*. Actually, we never lost.

Now, in my sixties, to get to sleep—*back* to sleep, banishing the dark disquietudes—I do something not dissimilar. I play imaginary tennis. For twenty minutes, sometimes more—for a time I wore a bracelet called a Jawbone Up, which monitored my sleep patterns and recorded how long I would lie awake—I take my own version of the yearlong men's pro-tennis tour. I play on my favorite courts around the world, ones at which I've sat over the years and watched the greatest players, watched with my wife or my son Luca or a close friend but mostly by myself, just me in a quiet, attentive crowd with a pen and notebook and a large bottle of water: exuberantly content. On my middle-of-the-night tour, I play in front of no crowds. I hit with Kirill. We don't play matches. He puts me through all the drills that we do for hours each week. I practice. I learn. And on the good nights I fall back to sleep a little better player than the night before, and with the sense that the practicing and learning and improving will go on and on, without end.

It begins, my fantasy tour, at Indian Wells, a March morning in the California desert, the valley-floor air dry and cool, the sun just above the Little San Bernardino Mountains to the east purpling the folds of the Santa Rosa Mountains to the west.

We are on a practice court, Court 3, at the southern edge of the tournament grounds, where I once watched Rafael Nadal hit buggy-whip baseline forehands one after another, dozens of them, working to calibrate his turbine-like topspin to the hot, arid conditions that can keep a ball sailing and sailing. I do a mini-tennis warm-up with Kirill. Soon enough, he hits a perfect backhand drop shot with enough underspin to bring the ball bounding back over to his side of the net after gently alighting on mine. I tap a clap of admiration on my strings, he catches my eye, smiles, and says: "Ready to go back?"

And, voilà! There we are in Paris, at Roland-Garros on the southern tip of the Bois de Boulogne, a sunny afternoon near the end of May, back a foot or two behind the slightly raised, white-tape baselines, the red clay smoothed and, in my mind, dampened by a morning shower to slow things down. We are on Court 2, old and intimate and a favorite because trees from the Bois can reach it with leaf-dapple and because the cement walls capture and amplify the song of properly struck tennis balls like no other place I've been. Kirill, at the center mark, has a hopper filled with new balls, and he is running me from corner to corner along the baseline, forehand then backhand for three or four minutes at a time, nonstop: me alternately hitting crosscourt and down-the-line; taking proper, short, sliding strides to the ball; moving back to deal with the high bounce off the clay; hitting my forehands with the kind of topspin and my backhand slices with the kind of bite I only pull off in my mind's eye in the middle of the night.

If this workout fails to get me back to sleep, we move on to Wimbledon. We are on the new No. 2 Court—an actual stadium but a smallish one, able to seat only four thousand spectators, which seems the perfect size to both create a sense of spectacle and allow for intimate tennis watching. And if you are in a seat high enough up on the court's north end—and it is an early evening in late June with a lot of light left in the day; and the second-round match you are watching has suddenly, after a tightly fought first set, turned into an ugly beatdown (2011: Juan Martín del Potro v. Olivier Rochus 6–7 (9), 6–1, 6–0, 6–4)—you can lift your head toward Wimbledon village. There, beneath a Constable sky, you can watch the play of sun and cloud-shadow off the spire of old St. Mary's Church, and—with the sound in the background of a tennis ball hissing on grass—think that life is very, very good. And if that vision isn't the last I see before nodding off, Kirill brings me to the net on Court No. 2 to practice volleying: forehand and back to ready position, backhand and back to ready position, overhead smash and repeat.

There are nights, thankfully few, when the tour has to be extended, and I move on to New York—to the Billie Jean King National Tennis Center in Flushing Meadows, Queens, a half-hour drive from my home in Westchester—and imagine a little more tennis, under the lights. Kirill and I are on Court 8, a field court, where, in 2010, as Labor Day weekend was beginning and New Yorkers were streaming out of town, I watched with a few hundred other fans—many, like me, by themselves—one of those matches that is no less compelling for being frayed, streaky, and inconsequential. Gilles Simon of France and the German Philipp Kohlschreiber had begun their second-round match in the late afternoon, but it was a nighttime match, the court inked in by dusk and the lights turned on, by the time they reached the middle of the fifth set in a match Simon eventually won. I make a point of watching both Simon and Kohlschreiber play whenever I can, though with their rankings almost never in the top ten, they are seldom on TV. Neither has an intriguing game, and

Simon is not a particularly likable guy—he may be the most sullen player of his generation. But both are under six feet tall and Simon weighs only 150 pounds or so—he's just a little bigger than me. (His French fans call him, presumably with affection, Le Petit Poulet.) I watch him, and Kohlschreiber, too, to marvel at how strong and fast and good someone my size is capable of being. The greatest men's players today, with their size, speed, and power, can seem to be only nominally playing the game I am striving to learn.

The Open's Court 8 is, in my mind, empty now, and, under the lights, Kirill begins serving to me. It's the drill we end each of our workouts with. The point is to get me to focus when I am tired—I'd have been hitting and running for ninety minutes now—and to speed up my reaction time. It's generally understood that the reaction time of a man in his sixties is slower than that of a man in his twenties, like Gilles Simon, and this is certainly true when responding to a tennis serve from Kirill, which can regularly reach 120 mph. There's so much for me to do: pick up the incoming ball (with my diminished eyesight); judge whether it has sidespin or is flat, with nearly no spin at all; decide whether I'll be hitting it back with a forehand or backhand, and raise my racquet and adjust my grip accordingly; and then *move* in order to be neither crowding the ball nor having to lunge for it.

I return scant few of Kirill's big serves. (When I do, he offers up his greatest compliment: "No way!") That's really not the point. No one I will play against can serve anywhere near as hard as Kirill. The point is to speed up my preparation and swing and for me to learn to concentrate even when I have next to no energy left—to "stay strong," as Kirill shouts at me from across the net. And, in the bigger scheme of things, I like to think as I wink off, the drill is designed to leave me humbled by a game I have come to play late in life and will never be *that* good at. It's a kind of bedtime prayer: I'm thankful to have discovered a passion that there is still enough time, maybe, to deepen through commitment, and, with it, an openness to a risk of failure that any passion demands.

10

I lost the first point I played at Forest Hills that Saturday morning, hitting a flat, crosscourt forehand too long, going for a hard winner, going for too much. I lost the next point, too, netting a backhand service return. But I won the next one, and the one after that on a clean, down-the-line forehand winner, and my opponent and I were tied, 30–30. That's when the skies opened, chasing us onto the veranda.

Geoff Cykman was his name. I had learned earlier that morning, thanks to Google, that he had long been the Bay Area's top senior player. I had known for weeks that he was the grass championship's sixty-and-over No. 1 seed. On the train and then the subway out to Forest Hills that morning—the train cars with a few young night-shift workers headed home; me in my tennis whites—I tried my best not to think about how good Geoff Cykman must be. I thought instead how cool it might be to win a game from him.

Geoff was my height, just shy of six feet, and slim. He wore glasses, and had sports heat patches affixed to his quads. We sat out the rain delay together and talked a little. Geoff's voice was soft, and he spoke carefully, pausing between his sentences and, at times, falling silent. Was he trying to stay focused on the match? (Should I have been?)

He was forthcoming in his way. He told me the high school he'd attended in San Francisco, George Washington High School, had been riven by racial tension in the late '60s, and he'd joined the tennis team, in part, to shelter him from that. He told me he'd sold his import-export business nine years ago because globalization had "cut him out." He and his wife were fine financially. He kept an eye on the stock market, he said, and wondered, but not too urgently, if he should be doing something more with his days. He mostly just played tennis now: at his club, the Olympic Club in San Francisco; at national and international tournaments; at Roy Emerson's tennis camp in Switzerland.

I knew within minutes of warming up with him how good he was—how much better a player he was than me. He was relaxed and consistent. Nothing about his strokes was overwhelming. But they were clean, efficient, with no apparent weakness on, say, the backhand volley. I was looking. I am sure he was looking, too.

By the time the shower had ceased and the courts were relatively dry, more than an hour had passed. We returned, warmed up, again, for five minutes or so, and resumed play. The match would not last long. Geoff won the first two points, and thus the game, and then another game, and another. I recalled Bob Litwin saying he would win three of every five points if he played a match against me. That's what Geoff was doing: winning three of five. He was doing it by making no unforced errors to my many, as I took risks and failed.

I never won a game. Twice, I took Geoff to deuce, and in one of those games, I was serving "ad in," up a point. I needed just one more point to win that game I coveted. I was mostly serving and volleying at this point in the match—down 0–3 in the second set—and was still losing most of the points. But the strategy had won me a few points, and the hustling toward the net had kept me focused and energized, my head up, undiscouraged. In my two previous games, I'd sliced serves wide to Geoff's backhand—slow, looping serves that provided me enough time to get close to the net to return his return with a sharp-angled, put-away volley. Both times he had sliced low, wickedly angled, crosscourt backhands, the ball passing me without my even grazing it with my racquet: beautiful, clean winners. *This* time, rather than following the path of my serve as I moved in to net—that is, veering slightly to my right—I came straight in, down the middle, to guard against his crosscourt return. And from there, I watched Geoff close his backhand stance, take the serve a fraction of a second later, and slice it low and hard down the line, behind me, three feet or more from my backhand reach. I lost the next two points, the following two games, and the match.

I see myself, now, smiling, and not ruefully, as I watched Geoff's backhand winner that thwarted my only chance of taking a game from him. And I certainly smiled as Geoff and I shook hands at the net after the match. I spent a long time in the shower after, thinking about how long and hard I had practiced to get to this point, and how far I had to go to get as good as I wanted to be. I also had the thought, and this made me smile, too, that tennis had become a sort of organizing principle of my life, a large part of who I was and how I went about my days. That really didn't depend on how good I was, or whether I won or not. It was not about outcomes. It was something I held in that indrawn part of me.

After I showered and changed into the street clothes I'd

brought along in a tote bag, I found a bench on the club grounds and called Alexandra, which I almost never did. It was a call I'd arranged with her beforehand. I thought it might be interesting to talk about the match with her and try to articulate what I was feeling about it.

"Hel*lo*?" she said in a singsong way.

"How do I sound?"

"So how did it go?"

"I got double-bageled," I said. "He was a really good player." Geoff went on to win the tournament, cruising through the draw, beating Victor Aguilar in his semifinal match 6–2, 6–1 before taking the championship final. He would end the year the No. 1 sixty-to-sixty-five-year-old player in the nation.

"I'm not humiliated, though maybe I should be," I went on to say. "I think what I am is humbled—if that makes sense."

"There's a difference between being humbled and being humiliated," Alexandra said. "Humiliation comes when a desire is mocked, when it is summarily shut down. When that happens, the space to learn and create collapses. But being humbled—that's valuable."

"Valuable how?"

"It's a reminder that there is something larger than you."

"Tennis. My attempt to get good at it."

"Yeah, it's inspiring, or can be, being humbled. It's a wonderful reminder that everything is a process."

There weren't enough hours left in my life to get good enough to beat Geoff Cykman, even if I used every one of those hours in an attempt to do so. There would come a day, and it could come tomorrow, when I would no longer be getting better at all. My game would stall, then diminish, like everything else. On my train home, that afternoon, that's what I found myself thinking about. It can be humbling to understand that a desire to learn something new, develop a passion, get good at something so late in life, is not going to ultimately thwart that stalling and diminishing, any more than it's going to lead to my thwarting the likes of Geoff Cykman.

You compete against it all anyway.

11

It requires body control, hand-eye coordination, quickness, flat-out speed, endurance, and that strange mix of caution and abandon we call courage," David Foster Wallace was contending, making the case for tennis being our most demanding sport. As if I needed reminding. I was rereading an essay of his called "Tennis Player Michael Joyce's Professional Artistry as a Paradigm of Certain Stuff About Choice, Freedom, Discipline, Joy, Grotesquerie, and Human Completeness," which Wallace had written for *Esquire* back in the 1990s. Rereading it as I was trying to take my mind off the fact that the prop plane I had boarded in Salt Lake City to fly south on a cool and cloudy October afternoon was getting harshly wind-batted above the Wasatch Range. In his too-brief life Wallace had come to observe tennis more ingeniously than any American writer ever had. I'd been an editor at *Harper's* when he published his first piece about tennis, a memoir we called "Tennis, Trignometry, Tornadoes: A Midwestern Boyhood." (He'd been a promising junior player.) And it was for a short-lived sports magazine, *Play,* which I'd helped to hatch as a spin-off of the *Times Magazine,* that Wallace wrote his last tennis piece, a remarkable—and remarkably long—meditation on

Roger Federer. (Its publication necessitated the combining of editing and tennis for me as nothing had or, I imagine, ever would. Wallace insisted on using a serial comma, which is not *Times* style, and threatened to withdraw the essay if he could not place commas before his many "ands." It went all the way to the top, to the executive editor, Bill Keller, who, amid his worries about reporters' safety in Afghanistan and the dwindling economics of newspapering, sighed and gave Wallace permission to punctuate as he pleased.)

I was heading to St. George, Utah, to a tennis camp, and I was bringing Wallace with me as an in-transit and mealtime and nightstand companion. Actually, it struck me while reading, or trying to, on the bouncing plane, that this trip might have made a good magazine assignment for Wallace. The camp I was heading to—the DFW-sounding Court Think Tennis Camp at Green Valley Spa—featured a video technology called Dartfish. I was going to be taped and get to watch my tennis game for the first time—taped and then analyzed. I'd been hitting for some time now, and thought it might be time to have a look at myself, or a look at myself from a new vantage, since looking at myself, scrutinizing myself, was a big part of what tennis was turning out to be for me. And the promise of Dartfish was that once you actually saw what you were doing—your footwork, your strokes—you would understand that what you were doing was not what you *thought* you were doing, and that therein lay a path to getting to a next level. Or, anyway, this was the wisdom, or a big part of it, at Green Valley, where the teaching was based on the principles of Vic Braden, by then in his eighties and a legendary instructor who had sought for decades to bring science and technology to bear on the improvement of tennis technique. I'd spend three days there, which, when you added in accommodations and the cost of getting to southern Utah from New York, was going to cost me around $2,500. As my plane descended over red-rock buttes and escarpments and a wide desert valley where a lot of '30s Westerns got filmed—a broodingly spectacular landscape gilded by an autumn sunset—the mute emptiness of the place, its far-awayness, reassured me: I was alone, and there was nothing better to do than indulge myself and play tennis.

The spa was situated on the western edge of St. George, which is not far from both the Arizona and Nevada borders. It's an area said to be home to poor Mormons, those for whom having children as teenagers has turned out as badly as it does most other places in the country, but with darkness having fallen by the time I retrieved my luggage, there was not much to see from the car that the spa had sent to fetch me. The spa itself turned out to be a modest compound of Santa Fe–style faux-adobe buildings and small, semidetached guest cottages arrayed around garden courtyards and swimming pools. And there was, too, a certain Santa Fe–style New Aginess to the vibe—a spacey friendliness at the front desk, books on yoga and spirituality in the gift shop, and, in the background, that electronic, down-tempo, modal-drone music that, to be honest, I find narcotically soothing.

I checked in, found my room (its décor more Laura Ashley than Santa Fe), unpacked, and, having pulled on a sweater, strolled, book in hand, to the dining room under a high, star-blanketed canopy. The dining room was mostly empty—a Sunday night? The post-banking-crisis economy?—but the tables were communal, and the point, the waitress who seated me said, was for guests to meet and interact. Ugh. I was steered to a big, round table where three women were finishing up their dinner. Actually, they hadn't finished up their dinner. The plates of apple slices they were slowly, slowly chewing and savoring *were* dinner! They had just arrived, too—from Salt Lake City, old friends, maybe ten years younger than me, who had been to Green Valley together before—and this was, for them, the start of a week of fasting, cleansing, dieting, stretching, meditating, walking, toning, pampering. . . . My arrival at the table had interrupted a conversation about the *Twilight* saga films and vampires.

"Did your wife see them?" one of the women asked. I assumed she had seen the wedding ring I was wearing.

"We don't have daughters," I said, hoping to preclude a *Twilight* follow-up and get quickly to some next topic, or none at all. "I'm here to play tennis."

"That explains it," one of the other women said. "You don't see men alone here. Men with their wives if they both could stand to lose some weight. I've seen that. But you don't need to lose weight. Gain a little, maybe."

This brought giggles all around. Maybe they were high from lack of food.

They were gone by the time my dinner arrived, off to some talk about wellness. I was the last person in the dining room, just me and my copy of Wallace's *A Supposedly Fun Thing I'll Never Do Again.* I ate half a roast chicken, with wild rice and a helping of kale, and drank a glass of Oregon Pinot Noir. Delicious, the food, the wine, Wallace's sentences, the being on my own with nothing ahead of me but three days of tennis playing. All my years married, decades, and I'd never done anything like this. I was alone in the middle of nowhere, just me and tennis. I required no thoughts of practicing with Kirill at Roland-Garros or Wimbledon to fall asleep.

12

I began my morning not on a tennis court but—in my whites and sneakers, my racquet in its sleeve at my side—in a small conference room turned into a classroom, seated in front of a whiteboard and a portable film screen. My fellow students, dressed for tennis, too, were a couple in their late thirties from Seattle, he a Microsoft senior manager, she a stay-at-home mom, and as we waited for our instructor to arrive and made small talk, they explained that they had always taken "active" vacations together and that they hadn't let the birth of their two children, the oldest having just begun elementary school, get in the way of that. The kids were with a nanny.

This immediately made them suspect in my eyes. I had inherited from my mother a belief that the world and everything in it conspired to harm your children, and that the only way to possibly prevent the worst was to never let them out of your sight. Barbara and I—because of my anxieties, not hers—had not left our sons to take a vacation alone until our tenth anniversary, when the boys were seven and five and we went off to Paris for five days. And even then they were with my parents. And even then I phoned the minute I got to the hotel. My mother explained that neither of the boys had any interest in coming to the phone, and that they were just fine, and the call was too expensive so don't call again. *Of course* they were fine, I fumed to myself after hanging up. She had them drugged with sugar and butterfat, and my father had TVs blazing in every room of their apartment, streaming cartoons and commercials for *more* sugar and butterfat.

Our instructor turned out to be Dave, the director of the camp. He was maybe ten years younger than me, solid, with a friendly moustache, a onetime minor-league ballplayer. He apologized to the Seattleites and me for running late, then told us we would spend the morning being introduced to some of the things Vic Braden had come to understand about the game. He began by saying that a tennis court was small in length and width, *very* small, smaller than we sensed. On a singles court—he was drawing a rough representation of one on the whiteboard—the difference between hitting a forehand down the line or crosscourt to the far corner—now he was tracing triangles inside his court—entailed changing the direction of your follow-through only 19.1 degrees. *19.1!*

"How, exactly, had Vic gotten it down to that point one?" I asked.

"Don't worry about that," Dave said. (He was right, but I'd come upon this observation of Wallace's over breakfast: "Unless you're one of those rare mutant virtuosos of raw force, you'll find that competitive tennis, like money pool, requires geometric thinking, the ability to calculate not merely your own angles but the angles of response to your angles.") The point, Dave went on to say, was that getting a ball to go where you wanted it to called for focus and precision, and that in envisioning your forehand, you should be trying to hit the ball as if you were sending it down a long, narrow sidewalk. And to do that you had to concentrate on extending your racquet farther out toward your target before completing your follow-through. Point your hitting palm directly at the target, he urged.

Dave went on to talk, convincingly, about how the net is higher than you think (more whiteboard geometrics) and about how hitting a forehand is as much a matter of verticality (lift) as horizontality (drive). His gift, I was coming to see, was the ability not to make things seem easier but to explain clearly that most everything about tennis was even more difficult than you thought.

We then watched a brief instructional film about the kinetic chain. This is the idea that, when hitting a stroke, in our case a forehand, the parts of the body should optimally act as a series of chain links, transferring energy up through the body to the racquet. Power was generated as follows: your bent legs rise, your torso rotates, your shoulder follows, your hitting arm comes around, and in the course of this sequence muscles are activated and elongated in a complex, biomechanical pattern called the stretch-shortening cycle. The end result, if you stretched all your muscles in sequence and on time, was that your racquet head speeded up. It was cool to watch this, I have to say. But then, the player in the film was young and expert, and he was making look effortless what you knew to be hard, and felt to be impossible.

After the film ended, Dave marched us out of class and toward a complex of machines like nothing I had ever seen before—not standard ball machines but batting cages for tennis, six of them, arrayed in a horseshoe shape. For the next forty-five minutes we hit and hit forehands, with Dave gently barking at us above the machines' din to bend our knees and "kiss the guns!"—that is, finish our swings with complete follow-throughs, the biceps of our hitting arms in our faces.

After an hour lunch break we were back to the forehand again, this time on one of the college's fourteen hard courts, where Dave arranged and rearranged orange plastic cones for us to direct our shots at. The Seattleites were proving good company, despite my early misgivings, and we ran and hit the afternoon away, encouraging one another and, while waiting our turns, marveling at the mountains, set against the blue, blue sky, to be glimpsed beyond St. George's valley subdivisions.

I smacked tennis balls for nearly four hours that first day—hit more forehands than I ever had in a week of lessons with Kirill and a match or two. My left shoulder and knees were sore, and after a shower, I treated myself to a ninety-minute, deep-tissue massage. And lying on the massage table, the New Age music gently droning, the massage therapist working my shoulder, I felt . . . I couldn't quite explain it to myself. Unburdened. Engrossed. Excited, but not anxiously so. *Happy.* Then it struck me: I was engrossingly, excitedly, happily *self-absorbed.*

The last twenty or so years of my life, I was thinking as my glutes got worked over, had been largely spent editing and parenting. This was true and not true, of course—I had been devoting a lot of time to tennis of late—but that's how it is with the story you tell yourself about yourself. I had worked most days helping writers and reporters make their pieces as good as they could be. I had spent evenings and weekends helping my sons to learn and grow. And when I wasn't doing those things I was spending a lot of time thinking about those things. Emerson said, "A man is what he thinks about all day"; I did think about things besides being an editor and a dad, but I was occupied and preoccupied with those roles, and encumbered by them, and thankful to be. That life, though, was giving way to another.

Here, at tennis camp, I was thinking about almost nothing

but tennis, about tennis and me. It was freshly, immensely pleasurable. It was also, I was aware, self-centered, *self*ish. Narcissistic? Alexandra and I had had a number of involved e-mail exchanges about the self and tennis and narcissism. I already understood that *narcissism* was a term that meant different things to different people, and that there was no general agreement on what it meant, even among those who wrote about it. While I'd been an editor at *Harper's,* one of the writers I worked with was the cultural historian Christopher Lasch, whose 1980 book, *The Culture of Narcissism,* became a much-discussed bestseller—though he thought most people completely misunderstood what he meant by *narcissism.* He went on to write a follow-up book, *The Minimal Self,* which was his attempt to clarify what he meant—that, essentially, Americans of many stripes were showing signs of what psycho-analysts describe as "pathological narcissism," harboring weak selves that needed constant validation. But Lasch continued to complain to me, as he complained to others, no doubt, that no one got it—that he was not ultimately concerned with '60s "permissiveness" or '70s hedonism. He thought the term *narcissism* might no longer be useful.

Alexandra also found the term limiting as a "type" because, as she put it once, "it's so reductive and pathologizing, like calling someone an hysteric." Another time, she explained to me (and why I had not figured this out on my own?) that it was natural to become more self-absorbed as we aged—as our kids went off and death edged closer, and as, with more years behind us than ahead of us, we got down to the knotty work of making sense of our lives, and maybe adding a new chapter or two. "That's not narcissism," she said. "That's, you know, set-ting the groundwork for possibility, change, growth—which is never easy, but especially later in life." In a later e-mail exchange, she went on to explain that there was a "healthy" narcissism everyone needed to call on in certain situations, and playing tennis was one of those. "Tennis players, alone on a court, have to maintain the illusion that they are in control of everything," she said. "They must also, to win, impose themselves on others." This required, at least within the confines of the court, a fair amount of self-regard, even grandiosity and—when you were down 1–5—magical thinking.

But if tennis took up a lot of your life—a lot of your thinking as well as your weekend afternoons—how could that narcissism be contained within the confines of a court? Having your glutes worked by a massage therapist miles from anything but tennis courts can get you, self-absorbedly, to thinking about such things.

13

Mirror neuron capacity is a term that brain scientists use. To have this capacity, as we humans do, means that the same region of the brain is in use whether we are performing an activity or, say, watching someone else perform that activity in a video. To some researchers, this means that watching is a great way to learn. In the years I have been playing tennis, especially with the advent of YouTube, I have called on this capacity a lot, and with great hopes. I watch slow-motion videos of Federer's serve, Wawrinka's backhand, the Bryan brothers' volleys. I watch over lunch at my desk at work, in crowded airport lounges, on my smartphone in line at the checkout counter. So it seemed logical to me that if I could see myself in a video, playing tennis, it would be an education. That's what had ultimately brought me to a tennis camp in southern Utah. And an education is what it turned out to be.

The Seattleites and I reported our second morning at camp to a court with a prefab shed behind the baseline on one end. There was a camera set up on a tripod, and Dave was inside the shed at a desktop, his brow furrowed. He was having some kind of problem syncing the cameras and the computer, and for the next hour or so, we students milled around. (There is a particular annoyance and agitation I feel when I'm waiting for something digital to do what it is supposed to quickly do.) When the Dartfish system was finally up and ready, things went swiftly and smoothly enough. We took turns hitting our forehands and backhands for the camera.

I concentrated especially on my slice backhand, since day two was going to be devoted to hitting from the backhand wing. It was the backhand I used almost exclusively when I was playing. Defensively, when I hit it on the run, its slow pace bought me time to get back to the middle of the court and into the point. Offensively, if I hit it low and with a bit of sidespin that, along with the backspin the shot demands, seemed to be a part of my shot, it forced my opponent to hit the ball awkwardly and up—an opportunity for me to approach the net for a volley.

There was some more waiting before Dave called the three of us into the shed. We huddled behind him as he sat at his computer, and soon enough we were watching video of our strokes. I joined in the gentle kidding, and tried to listen to Dave as he commented calmly on our form, or lack of it. But I was trying to mask a mood that was sinking toward black despondency. It had to do, in part, with how poor my technique was. When hitting my backhand slice, I was not always bending my knees. Or getting fully from my Eastern forehand grip to the Continental, though the distance was but one bevel. Or firmly cocking my wrist. Or swinging smoothly (I was, at times, stabbing at the ball). Or really engaging my hitting shoulder. Or following through enough—extending my arm out and then raising it after carving through the ball, the strings pointing up, my free arm rising with it to help maintain my balance—to consistently keep the ball from popping up.

But mostly what was darkening the morning for me, in

truth, was not my slice but simply seeing my aging self. It struck me that the last "me" captured on film was an eight-year-old, bending to field ground balls. My father had given up on home movies around then, and Barbara and I had no interest in videotaping our lives—not our wedding or our vacations or our kids (though there are plenty of photos of them). Now here I was, more than fifty years on, with skinny legs rising from big feet, shoulders scrunched beneath a too-large head, moving stiffly and, when striking a ball, contorting my creased and drooping face into hideous expressions of heed and strain. Because I was neither overweight nor balding, I had flattered myself that I looked younger than I was. Dartfish had disabused me of this. I did not. On Dave's computer screen, I looked every bit my age.

And a little older than that. The Dartfish system allows for the insertion—right there, on the computer screen, presto!—of a film clip of a tennis star doing what you have been doing, only correctly, and handsomely. Suddenly, there was Tommy Haas, the best-looking tennis player on earth, a man who had posed with his ridiculously attractive and curvy girlfriend (she became his wife) in a *Sports Illustrated* swimsuit issue, right in sync with me as we approached the ball, raised our racquets, and sliced our backhands. I mumbled something about being eager to get on the court and work on my backhand technique. Dartfish had taught me enough.

14

My last day at Green Valley, my Dartfish revelations behind me, was blissful, the hours of playing blurring together the way they must for kids who actually enjoy summer camp. We did all kinds of drills: approach-and-volley drills; a drill to practice overhead smashes in which you tap your racquet on the net, then sidestep or backpedal furiously, searching for the ball in the high sky; or, one of my favorites, the butterfly drill: my lefty forehand to Dave's righty backhand, his backhand down the line to my backhand, my backhand crosscourt to his forehand, his forehand down the line to mine. About butterfly drills Wallace wrote: "[O]nce the first pain and fatigue of butterflies are got through . . . a kind of fugue state opens up inside you where your concentration telescopes toward a still point and you lose awareness of your limbs and . . . whatever's outside the lines of the court, and pretty much all you know then is the bright ball and the octangled butterfly outline of its trail across the billiard green of the court." That was sort of the state I was in. The sun shone, Dave instructed, I ran and hit and heard the whoosh or thwock that signaled I was striking a ball cleanly, correctly—not half the time, but once in a while, which is to say, enough of the time.

Interestingly, not until the last hour of camp on day three did we actually play a game of tennis. "Adults—especially the types who show up at tennis camp—tend to be very focused on outcomes," Dave had said when we had dinner together the night before at the spa. "Wanting to win gets in the way of wanting to do things efficiently." Too true: I had immediately thought, when he told me that, of the six- and seven-year-olds I've watched taking lessons at my club, swinging and whacking balls, as instructed, with little regard for where they go or where they land, building muscle memory and securing approval, years away from the tightening and unease that come with keeping score.

No sooner had the four of us begun our set of doubles, with the warm, dry Utah afternoon beginning to cool as the sun made its way behind the mountains, than, with an aim to win, I was doing everything I had paid to be purged of. Dave never stopped admonishing me to bend and to follow through, and I never, or mostly never, got down on myself about it. Maybe it's easier to face your limitations—to face the fact that you will never be all that good, really—in a setting so lovely and so far from most everything, so far from the life that, for so many reasons, you've decided to make tennis a new and increasingly vital part of. "I submit that tennis is the most beautiful sport there is," David Foster Wallace wrote somewhere, and I was ready to submit, even amid those last shanked forehands and netted volleys, that my time at Green Valley brought that beauty closer, even as it confirmed how unobtainable it was certain to remain.

15

There is always something that feels a little odd about driving in your tennis shorts in December, especially if there are flurry remnants frozen to the bottom of your windshield and the late-afternoon sky is the gray of a charcoal-flannel suit. I had the seat-warmer on, and Arcade Fire's "Reflektor" blasting with the bass enhanced to try to get my blood flow thawed, as I navigated the maze of highways that years ago doomed the South Bronx. I was headed to Randall's Island and the Sportime tennis center, a state-of-the-art indoor facility and home of the John McEnroe Tennis Academy. My friend Paul and I were to play a match, as we had been doing so many Sundays for four, five years.

Among the many challenges of taking up tennis late in life is finding people to play with, especially during the winter (if you don't live in Florida or Arizona), when the nets are down and the tennis house shuttered at your club and there is no place to simply bump into someone who wants to play. But in truth it's a year-round dilemma. There are certain shared understandings you have to have with someone if you are going to regularly play a gladiatorial game against him. You want to be roughly the same level player—or, in my case, you may want there to be a player or two you hit with who is a little better than you, to raise your game. You want to play with someone whose temperament you are comfortable with; I like competitive types, but not screamers or racquet throwers or those who, in a tight game, consciously or not start calling any ball you hit near a line *out* ("hooking," as it is known). I also like playing with men with whom I can maintain a conversation that is not about tennis. During warm-ups, between sets, sitting around hydrating after a match, I like hearing about the work a man does, especially (to be honest) a successful man who feels, as I do, lucky at life; a tennis court is not a place to listen to complaints, disappointments, or even, by the etiquette of tennis, talk of a nagging ache or cold. It's hard enough to concentrate on defeating someone you *don't* feel sorry for. Tennis being a game played in large part by lawyers, doctors, and other professionals, it isn't too difficult to find men you enjoy talking with. It's getting all the aspects in one guy—the level of the game, the temperament, the conversation—that's hard, really hard.

I'm fortunate to have a number of such tennis pals now. They may come and go a bit—injuries, travel, or an ill parent may mean no tennis for weeks or months or even years. Only the afternoon before heading to Sportime to play Paul, I'd had a match with Ethan, a colleague of mine at the *Times* who I'd first met on court in a standing early-morning doubles game just a year after I began playing. He was a good player, with clean strokes and good legs, and when we'd played a singles match one morning back then, the result of the other regulars being unable to make it for the standing match, I hadn't won a game. Work took him to Israel for a number of years, and then, when he returned, he was hobbled by a knee injury. But we were playing again, and, for the first time against him, indoors on a cold, cold Saturday, I'd won in straight sets.

Unfolding over years, these matches against your tennis buddies—I've played scores of matches against Paul—have a way of measuring your game and, as they change, measuring you—how you handle winning and losing; how you handle a weakness of your game that an opponent has, over time, come to discover, and exploit; how *you* feel about exploiting a weakness you find in the game of a friend.

Paul arrived a bit late, having taken a taxi up from the loft he and his wife, Titia, had recently moved to in lower Manhattan. As was our way, we didn't say much before we played. We'd be on one of Sportime's hard courts, which Paul preferred. He knew John McEnroe's brother, Mark, who ran the tennis academy, and so was able to secure a court for us even on a busy Saturday afternoon. All around us, skilled teenagers were hitting with coaches, and the sound their heavy ground strokes were making was like music to me. Paul gave me a can of balls to open, and as he slipped out of his parka and picked up his racquet with his good hand, I felt, as I always did now, a pang of heart grief. And then, as I had taught myself to do, I found a place to set that aside. I was here to try to beat him. He'd want it no other way.

16

It was through my wife that I first met Paul. Barbara's love of art extends beyond the art history she researches and teaches, and through serving on an exhibition committee at our local art center, devoted mostly to mounting modest contemporary-art shows and providing art classes for children, she'd met Titia, a tall, no-nonsense Dutch woman who, in midlife, was pursuing a PhD in art history. They became fast friends and then great friends, discussing art over drinks and going into the city to hear lectures or try on dresses at Barneys.

Paul, Titia's husband, was not around much. He was living in Albany during the week, working for Governor Eliot Spitzer, first as budget director and then as director of operations, overseeing all New York's state agencies. When Spitzer resigned in the wake of a prostitution scandal, Paul stayed on in Albany as director of operations for Governor David Paterson, but was soon back in Westchester, working in the financial-products group at Bloomberg. When I got to know him at a couple of dinner parties early in 2009, he seemed to be pondering what to do next with his life. He was a couple of years younger than me, boyishly lean and angular, bespectacled and driven. He had, I would come to learn, a not misplaced sense that he knew more than most of the people gathered at any table with him about just about anything, though he was careful never to dominate a conversation. He would listen and frown, which for some reason delighted me. He was trained as a lawyer but had made a good deal of money as a managing director at Merrill Lynch and as a CFO of Priceline, and was now really interested only in public service, which he planned to get back to. He cared about writing; he funded a chair at Yale for the teaching of the essay. Unlike anyone else leaving my home after dinner on a Saturday night, he was going to get up the following morning and head to church. His faith—and it was faith, not simply habit—intrigued me.

He had been playing tennis since high school. When summer came, we arranged to play at the local country club, where he was a member. His shots were cleaner than mine, his serve harder. I played uglier but ran faster. Paul won the first match we played, and the next, and the next. But they were close, hard fought. We got into the habit of playing late on Sunday afternoons and then, after showering, heading to my house or his, where Barbara and Titia would join us for drinks or dinner. Their two children, like ours, were teenagers who might, or more often might not, join us. They would all be college students within a couple of years—each of our oldest already was—and we, the grown-ups, were aware (I very much was) of a transition in our lives of which these evenings represented—the best of what suburban living with no children around, and the rest that comes with aging, could hold: pleasure, quiet and warm.

I was picking up the etiquette of tennis from Paul, learning how to be fiercely competitive in a gentlemanly way. I learned those gracious on-court phrases—the serve "just back"; the passing shot "too good"; the "sorry," however insincere, after a ball you've struck slaps the net cord and somehow has enough momentum to just eke over the net, irretrievable—that soften the failures and disappointments of tennis. I glimpsed for the first time how cruel tennis could be—how in the breach you inevitably worked to exploit your opponent's weakness: my backhand, his fatigue. I felt within myself the kind of mid-match mood swings I'd seen in the tennis players I watched on TV, the confidence giving way to doubt and frustration, and then, on good days, the confidence reemerging from somewhere: a second, psychological wind. We pushed each other, and discovered things about each other, and ourselves. I started slowly, tentatively, anxiously, every match, as if I didn't belong on a tennis court. Paul had a hard time closing, was prone to double faults when serving for a match, and if he lost, which he did a couple of times by summer's end, he would not speak to me directly after, but walk to the parking lot alone—though be relaxed and talkative an hour or two later with our wives and cold white wine.

I had found a tennis rival. And more important to me, I had made a new friend, no easy thing later in life. I sensed the tennis was speeding up and deepening our understanding of who we were, temperamentally and characterologically. That fall and into the winter, as we drove to indoor courts to play, we talked with surprising ease about big things, philosophical issues, the way the world worked, and didn't. We were in something together.

When Andrew Cuomo ran for governor, Paul signed on. He wrote white papers, provided advice on energy, the state economy, and other issues. He went back to Albany after Cuomo was elected. As the state director of a new agency and the chair of a new commission, he was charged with figuring out how the state government might be reinvented. He worked ceaselessly in 2011 but did find time to hit with a pro in Albany and to play a weekend match with me a couple of times a month. He and Titia had also bought a second home on the Maine island of North Haven, and when the renovation was completed that summer, Barbara and I drove up for a weekend. There was a Har-Tru court up an unpaved road just a short walk from the house, and before lunch on Sunday, Paul and I played a match. It was a beautiful August morning: the sky azure, the waters of the nearby inlet sun-spangled, the view inland firred, the air touched with evergreen and salt. And Paul played as well as he had ever played against me, neither tiring nor wavering, beating me 6–2, 6–2.

17

It was the first thing I thought of—Paul, sweat-soaked and smiling at the net, the quick but not meaningless post-match handshake and embrace we tennis players do—when Barbara phoned me at work one morning early the following January. She was crying. Titia had phoned her from Holland, where she was visiting family. Paul was in the hospital in Albany. He had driven himself there, hours after the governor's 2012 State of the State address and the parties that followed, and then collapsed. His small intestine had perforated; sepsis was coursing through his body. He was now in an induced coma and his chances were bleak.

In the days that followed, Barbara joined Titia in Albany, and one night she called just as I had arrived home from work and asked me one of those questions that no amount of lived life can prepare you for. The doctors had talked to Titia, and Titia had talked to her—what she was saying was headed somewhere dreadful, I could tell—and they, Titia and Barbara, had concluded that I would know, or might, if anyone could: If gangrene from the septic shock spread to Paul's limbs, and they had to amputate his arms and maybe a leg, maybe two, would he want to live?

I was old enough, and self-conscious enough, to know that we all are capable of acting in clichéd ways in overwhelming moments, and that clichés are not empty for being clichés, not at all. I told Barbara I'd call her back, set down the phone, lit a fire in the fireplace, poured a Scotch, and stared. I thought of all that tennis Paul and I had played, Paul darting around the court, swinging his racquet in smooth, well-honed arcs, all that bounding aliveness heightened by the court's confinement. I stared into the fireplace, drank some more, and began to weep. Did those baselines and sidelines that held us in our weekly game, summoning, compressing, and releasing our energies, also create the illusion that they walled off the world, its own forces and terrible turns?

So literature has taught. I drank and fed the fire and found myself thinking of Nabokov's autobiography, *Speak, Memory*; of the clay court his father had had built on the family's country estate outside St. Petersburg, edged by pea-tree hedges and reached via an alley of slender oaks, its lines repainted each morning by Dmitri, the dwarfish gardener, who would also appear with umbrellas should the family game be interrupted by a cloudburst. It was that image—that lovely, moneyed ease—that, with the Nabokov estate, the Bolsheviks would soon enough destroy. And then there is Giorgio Bassani's *The Garden of the Finzi-Continis,* and the little court tucked amid the trees of the Finzi-Continis' stately grounds, where the college-age sons and daughters of Ferrara's best Jewish families, now banned from the tennis club by racial laws, played on warm fall afternoons in 1938 and nibbled on tiny *buricchi* from the city's best kosher pastry shop—incapable of imagining, despite their anxieties, that most of them would, five autumns on, be deported and murdered in German death camps.

I poured more Scotch. I had no idea what Paul would want. He was more resilient than I, I sensed, and he did have religious faith, though that could cut either way with the question at hand. The only real gauge I had was me: What would *I* want were my arms and legs to be taken from me? I sensed—no, I *knew*—that, were it me, I would want to die. How sure I was of that, suddenly, and how strange, in a way, that I would be. Death-haunted, and increasingly so, I had never been able to contemplate dying, my dying, for very long. It was fear, of course, that kept me from going there, but, for some reason, the fear was not creeping up this time. Was it the Scotch, followed by another? Or that near-giddy lightness that sometimes visits you after you have had a long cry? I *was* living so much in my body now, I remember thinking. That's who I had become. As ridiculous as it sounded, even to me, it had become my quest to become a tennis player. There was simply no way I would want to go on without the running, the moving, the physical freedom. (As will happen when I've been drinking, philosophical flotsam surfaced, Kierkegaard: "Health and salvation can only be found in motion.") Thinking of Paul, and our tennis, I, for the first time in my life, found myself considering my own death with a calm frankness—not that the fear did not soon again begin making its regular 3 a.m. visits.

18

Paul's legs would be spared, it turned out. He remained unconscious for nearly two weeks. He underwent nine surgeries during that time. The surgeons later told him that each of those days might have been his last, and that several of them, by all rights, should have been. One of those surgeries took much of his left arm. And later operations would remove many of his toes.

Nine months later, at summer's end, we were, miraculously, on a tennis court again, Paul and I, in North Haven. There would be no match; there would never again be the kind of tennis we had played. His body had been put through too much, he had one arm, and, in the years, to come, I would be devoting even more time and energy to improving. But he had legs, moving gingerly now with few toes, and he had his right arm to hold and swing his racquet. And on that afternoon he had a new, custom-built prosthetic device. In place of the steel hook he strapped on most mornings now was a flesh-colored hand—cupped to hold a tennis ball for serving!

We rallied from the baselines at first, tentatively. In my mind I was trying with my returns to find a place between going for the corners and simply pushing the ball back and up the middle—between cruel and condescending. Not that I could make balls go just where I wanted them to go. Retrieving and picking up balls were not easy for Paul; he'd have to bounce a ball up from the ground with his racquet, a standard enough on-court trick, then get his racquet under it quickly and tap it up to waist height, then hit it my way. After ten, fifteen minutes, though, we fell into a pretty good rhythm, and Paul's low, backhand slice seemed as strong (i.e., as unreturnable to my backhand side) as ever.

Then we paused and Paul asked me to help him readjust the prosthetic. The harness that held it in place was cutting into his shoulder. I pulled off his tennis polo and saw for the first time his torso, post-surgeries. He looked like the victim of a mad knifer. How his body had withstood the assault I had no idea.

Paul wanted to play some points. He was never one for just hitting around, or for doubles, for that matter, and that was not going to change, I was to understand. Singles tennis was what measured things. I stood back to receive, the sun on my back, and watched my friend toss a ball skyward with a length of molded plastic. It didn't always work, or, in truth, even mostly work. But it did work from time to time, and held out the promise of working better eventually, and for Paul that was plenty enough for an afternoon in late summer, and more than enough for me, too.

And we kept at it, Paul and I. He worked on his game with a teaching pro when he could, and moved better on hard courts with his missing toes than on clay. When his prosthetic cooperated and his service toss went up straight, which it was doing now more and more, the result was still a serve that gave me fits on my backhand. That wintry afternoon at Sportime was filled with longish rallies and deuce points, and when I eventually won, 6–3, 6–3, it felt good, the way winning always does. But not as good as playing, still scrambling and fighting and playing.

19

'd first read about Brian Gordon in *Tennis* magazine—about his outdoor laboratory in Boca Raton, at the Rick Macci Tennis Academy, and his quest to use digital technology to capture information about a player's strokes and then, with the help of software he'd developed, analyze the biomechanics of everything that player was doing, much of it wrong. Gordon was a longtime tennis coach and a serious research biomechanist, and he came across as an exuberant believer in the potential of data to reveal the inner secrets of a player's tennis game and point the way to improvement. Even *my* game. Though, in truth, Gordon mostly worked with those kids, teenagers and younger, sometimes considerably younger, who dream of being a touring pro or at least a Division I college player; who practice five or six hours a day; who get homeschooled in the south Florida condos into which their families have moved from the suburbs of Boston or somewhere in Belarus in order that their child can play high-level tennis; and whose development Gordon monitored digitally and fussed over on-court year-round.

Tennis at the top level has its metrics now: percentage of first-serve points won, number of unforced errors on the backhand side . . . None of these sorts of things were tallied, or mattered much, at the level where my game resided. But what Gordon measured intrigued me. He and his software gave your shots a detailed physical exam. Think of it as a biomechanical MRI or X-ray and diagnosis of who you were, physically, as a tennis player.

When I drove to the Macci Academy the first time from my hotel near the beach, I discovered that the frontier of tennis technology was cordoned by a chain-link fence, tucked in a corner of the academy, and protected from the elements by a yellowed canopy, a stretch of it torn away by one or another tropical storm. It was an open-air tinkerer's garage, and that's where I found Gordon on that tropically pallid morning. He was staring a little anxiously at a laptop resting upon a small plastic tray-table when I peeked into his place through a gate. He turned, smiled, and then slowly waddled toward me, a bear of a man in tennis clothes and a sun-faded baseball cap. "Arthritis in both my hips," he said, after shaking hands. "I played contact sports, football and hockey, but all the injuries, all the surgeries: tennis. Tennis takes it out of you."

The lab was essentially a hard-surface tennis court with a tall cement wall bisecting it along the net line. In front of the wall, on the half-court where Gordon conducted his tests, were two large, oval-shaped golf nets—positioned to capture the balls I was soon to hit. There were wires running every which way, and pieces of tape crisscrossing the baseline: It was like upstage at an off-off-Broadway theater. And arrayed around and above on steel poles were ten high-speed cameras, each, Gordon explained, capable of capturing four hundred frames per second and each emitting infrared light.

He was almost ready to go, having gotten here at dawn, he told me, to get all the cameras set up and synced with the software he'd developed. With him, helping out, was his intern, a seventeen-year-old player under his tutelage, Remi Ramos. Tennis had taken its toll on her, too, recently: She'd been a nationally ranked junior, and, according to the website of Tennis Recruiting Network, had attracted the interest of Columbia, Tufts, and Georgetown. But the previous fall she'd torn her hip, which required surgery, and now, about to enter her senior year of high school (through homeschooling), she was planning to rehab and train for a year before attempting to attract once again the interest of college tennis coaches.

Remi helped me get suited up. First I wiggled into a black, bodysuit-tight, short-sleeve nylon pullover, struggling to get it over my tennis polo. Almost immediately, the morning felt hotter. The tight, black top was pocked with small, spherical, reflective markers, and so were the Velcro bands Remi affixed to my arms and legs. There were also markers on a cap I was given to wear, and still more markers were taped to my sneakers and my racquet: fifty-nine in all.

It's complicated, but what would occur while I was hitting tennis balls was that the infrared light emitted by the cameras would bounce off the markers and be reflected back upon the cameras' lenses. More than one camera would receive the reflection of a given marker as I moved through my strokes, and this would allow for the creation of 3-D imaging. This 3-D imaging, in turn, would provide Gordon and his software what he needed to create stick-figure animations of my swings. And from this, and the visual data collected by the rapid-fire cameras as they traced my swings—data that Gordon's software would turn into numbers and graphs—I would learn almost everything there was to learn about my strokes: in short, *everything I was doing wrong.*

"Here's the deal," Brian announced. (Over the course of five days and many hours with him, he began only two or three sets of instructions or trains of thought without saying that.) We would start with my forehand. He crouched behind one of the golf nets, pointed me toward a piece of tape maybe three yards to the right of the baseline's center mark (to the right, because I am left-handed), lobbed a ball toward the center line, and I slide-stepped toward it and whacked a forehand. I quickly slid back and repeated this a dozen times. Then, without pausing, I moved to the left side of the center mark and hit a dozen or so slice backhands on the move, followed by a similar number of backhand drives. Gordon lobbed and ducked and offered nothing but encouragement as I swung away. I ended with ten or fifteen serves. It had taken five, six minutes. I was sweating profusely and feeling the apprehension I've felt when I've taken a stress test.

20

It was going to take Brian a few hours to turn the raw foot-age his cameras had captured into data and graphs of my strokes. He suggested I return at lunchtime with sandwiches, and we could sit and go through his findings together. I drove ten minutes into downtown Boca, a small grid of low-slung neo–Spanish Mission storefronts, and, after walking around for twenty minutes, found a gourmet meat shop. It turned out they didn't make sandwiches, but the butcher behind the counter enthusiastically directed me to a place out on one of the strips, V&S Deli, which to his mind made the best sand-wiches I would find for miles around. I got back in my rental car, drove another ten minutes, and had no problem finding V&S's: There was a line out the door.

It took me a half hour to make my way inside, and when I did, it was like stepping back into my childhood: Sunday morning, after church, my father and I at Romano's, he choos-ing the cold cuts that my mother would fill his sandwiches with and pack each night into a lunch pail with a thermos of coffee: mortadella, Genoa salami, pancetta. Here at V&S's, as at Romano's fifty years ago, were the maps of Italy on the walls, along with framed, autographed glossies of Frankie Avalon and Dion, now joined, of course, by ones of the *Sopranos* cast. There was the banter about sports and family and the perils of eating too much—always, in the end, dismissed—among the countermen and their customers. But for me, mostly, there were the aromas: cheese-pungent, vinegary, garlicky, herbaceous.

Ethnicity has never meant much to me, and it makes me uneasy, and always has, when I encounter someone for whom it seems to mean a lot. Ethnic pride was something I saw Italian-Americans developing in the late '60s, after blacks began clamoring for black power and the counterculture threatened working-class ways. (Before that, the Italian-Americans I knew mostly talked about being Sicilians or Piedmontese or, in my case, Lombards—distinguishing themselves from *other Italians*.) The newfound ethnic pride was reactive, and too often smolderingly angry and bigoted. But food, Italian food: It's always, to me, meant warmth, comfort, delight.

So why was I uneasy, at the familiar, familial counter of V&S's? I knew, or thought I knew, immediately: I was in tennis whites. I felt clammily self-conscious. There was something . . . what? Out of place? Imposterish? I found myself thinking: Had I come to love tennis as a rejection of a world I'd mostly left behind when I left for college? Or: Had I taken up tennis late in life to prove it was not simply the well-born elite who could play it?

I caught myself: You are someone who hates waiting on lines, and your mind is taking itself off that. I had never rejected my past. I had simply gone to school, taken an editing job, and discovered I loved it, and done it well enough to put myself in a position to get lucky. And I had nothing to work out with the elite, at least as far as I could tell. For that matter, I was not at all sure what an "elite" was anymore. It surely had little to do with tennis now. Tennis, at my club and throughout America, was a pastime mostly of the affluent and educated, true. It was not a game played much in impoverished neighborhoods or trailer parks. But it's been a long time since it was exclusively a game of blue bloods. Atlanta was the city where the largest percentage of men and women and kids played tennis, and they tended to be black and white and to play on public courts. Still, it was true that the whites I was wearing—that my club required—were a vestige of a different time, when tennis was an upper-crust pursuit.

What I mostly think is that entering an Italian deli in tennis whites, the juxtaposition of place and out-of-place, was an unsettling reminder to me of how far I was, in so many ways, from the world of my boyhood. Here, unsuspectingly, alone in a south Florida strip mall, I had inhaled and—like *that*—had one of those vertiginous moments when you become too aware of time's passing. The tennis whites magnified the distance between now and then. The sheer velocity of life! You make your way in the world; you move on; you change; you again and then again reach for something new—and then you find yourself, out of nowhere, at a place that provides a vantage point on the time that has sped by, the distance you have ventured, for better but never only for better. I gulped a Limonata like a boy, and, when my turn came to order those sandwiches (which would turn out to be so delicious), made small talk with the counter guys about pickling vegetables, which my father had done, storing them in big jars kept on the refrigerator door.

21

I bumped into Brian in the parking lot of the academy coming back with the sandwiches, and, under threatening skies, we headed into an office in the tennis house to go over what he'd gleaned about my strokes. Setting up his laptop, Brian told me a little about himself. He was fifty-two, and lived with his wife in a rented condo near the beach. He had attended Colorado College, where his father taught, and had then moved on to the University of Colorado at Colorado Springs, enrolling in a new, interdisciplinary master's degree program in exercise science. He was already coaching tennis, and this was fueling his interest in biomechanics. He came to believe that there was a most efficient way, an optimum way—a *right* way—to do most everything in sports, and that if you could capture accurate data about the approaches and techniques of the very best players, and have that to compare with data retrieved from young, developing players (or, in my case, aging, developing players), you could have scientific *facts* to work with and to chart improvement.

He eventually earned a PhD in biomechanics from Indiana University, all the while continuing to coach tennis, he recounted to me, and, for a time, working with swimmers

training for the U.S. Olympic team in Colorado Springs, pho-
tographing their strokes and kicks with underwater cameras.
He'd set up shop at Macci's academy three years ago. "Thing is,
I've had these ideas for quite a while," he said. "But it's sort of
been a matter of waiting for technology that was fast enough
and accurate enough to get the data."

A torrential shower was now darkening the afternoon, providing what I considered a suitable sense of foreboding, and
I was about to get an evidence-based diagnosis of my game.
Brian was gentle, sort of: His data had showed him that my
strokes, all of them but my backhand slice, were, to him and
his data, "a bit of a mess but not unfixable." What he'd walk
me through in detail was my forehand—"I really like some
things I'm seeing there"—and then we'd meet on the court the
following morning and he'd begin to show me how he thought
it could be made better.

With the tap of a keystroke, a version of me out of some
'80s computer game popped up on the screen: spaghetti-strand
torso, arms and legs, swinging away and depicted from the
side, back, and above. The first thing I noticed was my stance.
I'd thought I began my forehand from a traditional closed
stance, my right shoulder pointed toward the net. Most top
pros hit from an open stance, squarely facing the net, the ball
coming back at them now too quickly for them to have time to
turn to the side. I was starting my forehand from somewhere
in between, a so-called neutral stance, and Brian liked that.

He also liked—again, unbeknownst to me until now—
that I wasn't bringing my racquet all the way back behind
me, that I had a compact swing and kept my racquet away
from my body, "outside." "That's a hard thing to teach, but
for some reason you're there," he said. (I tried to take that as
a compliment.) With the setup I had, he explained, I could

and should be hitting an "ATP forehand" (ATP being the Association of Tennis Professionals, comprised of the top men's players) with a "windshield-wiper finish" (the racquet finishing its swing in a sweep across my body). Some version of that is what you see Roger Federer and the rest using: the swings compact, the racquet whipping past their torsos, rather than the longer, more traditional circular, low-to-high, brush-up-the-back-of-the-ball, finish-over-the-shoulder swing you still see in the woman's game. But to swing that way—the ATP way—I had to learn to use my body more, Brian said. And I wasn't using my body much at all.

Brian then took me through a series of data visualizations—tables, charts, bar graphs, interactive graphs—that showed precisely what my hitting arm, left shoulder, legs, and trunk were doing, and when, during the seven-tenths of a second it took me to execute a forehand stroke. My setup was good enough, my knees bent, my racquet head up off my left hip. I did need to move my racquet head more to the outside as I began my forward swing: eight or nine degrees, according to Brian's understanding of the ideal, which he arrives at by analyzing biomechanical data and studying film of today's tennis greats. I also needed to firm up my wrist. And to straighten my elbow more.

The real problem, though, was between my knees and neck: The "angular speed" of a player's hips during a forehand swing should, Gordon believes, be about four hundred degrees per second, but mine was only half that, according to what his cameras captured. The same went for my upper trunk. (Goal: 800 d/s. Me: 432.) Moreover, the torso turning I was doing was coming at the end of my forward swing, after I'd turned my shoulder, brought my arm through, and begun contacting the ball, not at the beginning, when it could provide power:

A remarkable rolling graph of my swing made this damningly clear. I wasn't uncoiling the "kinetic chain"—knees-to-hips-to-torso-to-shoulder-to-racquet—that could give my forehand pace. I was *arming* the ball.

Brian then tapped another key and up came a super-slow-motion video of a young Federer (he still sported a stubby ponytail) hitting a baseline forehand from a neutral stance. "He's starting pretty much where you are," Brian observed, and we both cracked up. Fed finished his swing, and Brian replayed it several more times before closing his laptop. "Here's the deal," he told me as we got up to leave. "Tomorrow we're going to try to start building a forehand for you more like that."

22

It was about halfway through the fourth time we'd repeated the baseline drill with the medicine ball that I concluded that I was never meant to be an athlete. I had been trying to remain positive: *You're escaping January in New York. Your forehand, your best shot, is going to get even better.* But it didn't feel like things were going according to plan. The plan was to spend a week with Brian as if I was one of the ten- or twelve- or fourteen-year-olds attending the academy—as if I were *promising*.

As if.

It wasn't that I was tired, though I was. My legs were out of bounce. The south Florida sun had baked away my focus. I was gasping for whatever oxygen there was in the stifling stickiness.

And it wasn't that I wanted to quit. I just don't do that. I like persevering. (Maybe it was the deep hold Catholicism had on me as a boy.) I'd been on the court for more than three hours, and I wasn't done, and that was fine—I'd do what Brian asked of me, or try.

"Stop coming up!" he barked. "Everything you are doing today is coming up—legs, torso, swing. Don't want to be coming up. Don't want to be straightening. What you want is to be twisting and flipping those hips. Stay down and twist!"

No, it wasn't my body telling me I would have never had it to be an athlete. It was the presence of these young kids on the courts surrounding me as I heaved the medicine ball. They *were* athletes. Their presence—their speed and grace and power—seemed a reproach. Or my presence seemed an embarrassment.

I signaled to Brian I needed some water, and took a few moments to right myself. I wanted to live in my body *now*, I reminded myself, in my sixties, before the sad smalling down, when it would no longer be so easy (or worse). But as much as I admired these kids and their honed ground strokes, I would *not* have wanted to live that way, so narrowly and intensely, at the age of eight, or ten, or twelve—when it would have had to happen in order for me to actually become an athlete. I would have never mustered the discipline back then. I would have resented the sacrifice. I would have been daydreaming of biking aimlessly or longing to be lost in a Bond novel or new Beatles album.

I recalled a conversation I'd had with Kirill: "You wouldn't have liked being a tennis player like me," he'd said. I immediately suspected that he was right—he is about so many things. (You do come to trust a coach, I knew even from my brush with organized sports in high school—and even if this coach was young enough to be my son.)

"Why's that?" I'd asked.

"You hit a point where it is work, and you only want to put in the work if you have this end goal of being a top tennis player. Then you actually like the work. You . . . I mean, you love tennis—but I can't see you, you at twelve or fourteen, having that goal. It's just not who you are."

Christ, get focused, I told myself as I drank a little more water and Brian checked his phone. *Be. Here. Now,* I whispered, not without a little irony (as ever), as I tend to whisper when my mind wanders (as ever), as I have whispered to myself since my college days, when we read Ram Dass. I got back on the court and the drill continued. And Brian went back to offering his comments and correctives, exhorting me to stay down—knees bent, up only on the balls of my feet—as I continued to slide-step from the center notch of the baseline to the left corner, there to meet the ten-pound medicine ball that he was hurling from the middle of the backcourt, "no-man's-land," ten feet away. I was to catch the ball with two hands outstretched to my left, swing my arms back, do a shoulder turn as if I was setting up for a forehand, and toss the ball back hard to Brian—rotating my hips to generate power and carry my arms forward to throw—before slide-stepping back toward the center to begin again. Ten times without stopping, I was to do this. I think I was up to seven or eight.

This is a plyometric exercise, plyometrics, essentially, being exercises that are built upon the idea that it's good for your muscles to exert maximum strength for as short a time as possible. The goal is to improve performance, not conditioning. You jump up on boxes and jump down to work your lower body. You catch medicine balls and toss them back to work your upper body. Plyometrics were the thing just then among serious tennis players who wanted to improve their quickness and racquet-head speed. And here I was, in Florida, trying to act like a serious tennis player.

The medicine ball was only part of the drill. First Brian had me do the slide-step thing with my racquet, ten times, stopping at the corner to hit crosscourt forehands with the tennis balls he was tossing me. Then ten times with the medicine ball. Then I would swing (ten times) something called an Etch-Swing (named after its designer, Pat Etcheberry, a renowned tennis trainer); an Etch-Swing looks like a stickball bat with propeller blades attached to its end: It creates wind resistance as you swing. (Imagine swinging a weighted baseball bat that grows heavier the harder you swing.) Then the racquet again. Then back to the medicine ball. Then, finally, one last time with the racquet. It's kind of exhausting just to write that and read it over. I was doing it three or four times in the course of a day spent mostly on court.

I was trying to get my hips and torso turning earlier and trying to allow my laid-back hitting arm to be carried forward by the rotation of my body. But I couldn't quite get it, despite the hours of drills devoted to instilling muscle memory. "All this emphasis you have on the arm," Brian muttered. "It's a control thing, this feeling you have of needing to be in control." (All tennis coaches are shrinks, too.) "Let go, man. Let *go*!"

I did. My forehands were spraying every which way—to the far fence and an adjacent court and, many times, into the bottom of the net—but they were hard and, even with my Eastern grip, had topspin generated from the clockwise rolling of my arm that culminated in the across-the-chest follow-through. Brian approached me and took hold of my non-hitting arm, extending it along the baseline; I had been pointing it at the incoming ball, as many players do. He told me that holding my arm the way he positioned it would help me hold my upper torso and shoulder back until my hips had first engaged and cleared.

The spraying of balls continued. I didn't know how much longer I could stay focused, and my shoulder and forearm were beginning to ache. I held up my hand to signal *enough,* and Brian smiled. "Not bad," he offered.

We grabbed some water, sat down on a courtside bench, and talked a bit. At one point, I asked him what his technology was doing for his developing students that simply pointing things out to them on court, as he had been doing with me for hours, could not do.

He explained that the data he gathered allowed him to chart a player's development over time—to build a statistical memory bank. He also told me that he believed such data helped a player better understand that power was less a matter of raw strength than of refined mechanics.

"Here's the deal: I believe that if you understand why you should do something, you buy into it, and then it's easier for you to do it," he said. "Scientifically measuring your development and interpreting it—that reinforces the understanding."

And, with this understanding, how good could a sixty-year-old player like me get?

"Not all that good," he said, and slapped my back and laughed. "But you *would* get better. And be less prone to injury. And you'd have this sense that you were hitting a ball with the best techniques we know of now. What's wrong with that?"

23

On the third day of my January week at the academy, I arrived early and pulled into a space alongside one of the practice courts. It was a gray morning, windy, thin rain spitting every now and then from the cottony, quick-moving clouds. I wasn't to meet Brian for another forty-five minutes, so I sat in my rental car and watched a girl becoming a twenty-first-century tennis athlete.

She was nine or ten. She had on a pink tennis dress with a matching visor, a long and braided blonde ponytail arranged to weave just so out the back of the visor and make its way down much of her back. She was not tall. She was lithe and, I glimpsed soon enough, quick and strong.

She was returning serves in the deuce court from a coach with a basket of balls. Another coach was behind her, filming her returns. Her mother, or so I presumed it was, was watching from the far side of the court, addressing the girl every so often in Russian. Rick Macci himself was on the court, alongside the girl, his arms crossed, watching. (Macci had coached Serena Williams when she was a girl; that fact continued to lend his attention an allure.) Again and again, for twenty minutes or more, she crouched at the baseline; spun her racquet in her right hand; took an exaggerated split step as the coach doing the serving was about to make contact with the ball; then moved into the court, her racquet back and poised, to take the serve early, "on the rise," with a shortened, explosive forehand before the bounce got too high. The coach was serving kick serves, which are designed to bounce high, and on those occasions when the girl did not get to the ball early, it bounded above her visor.

There was something riveting about it—the girl's drive and ability. Her form on the forehand return was smooth, whippy, lovely. She hit cleanly, with considerable pace. I doubt very much if I could have won if we played a match.

But what was she giving up to get that good that young? I found myself thinking of an essay my psychotherapist-friend Alexandra had e-mailed me, written in the '50s by D. W. Winnicott, the influential English psychoanalyst who was also a pediatrician by training. It was titled "The Capacity to Be Alone," and in it, Winnicott argues that in order for a child to properly develop, he or she must be able to feel alone in the presence of the mother. For Winnicott, there was something profoundly important about the early experience of being in the company of somebody so consequential to you without being impinged upon by her demands, and without her needing you to make a demand on *her.* If you, as a child, could pull this off, Winnicott believed, you could forget yourself, absorb yourself in a game, say, or a book. You could, in time, *become* a self.

Alexandra had sent me the essay after we'd been e-mailing back and forth about the healthy aloneness singles tennis affords—and about its affinities with reading, my life pursuit. Now, watching this young girl whacking her service returns, I wondered: How much aloneness was tennis affording her?

How was she becoming herself? Where was the space for that? Her days were essentially hour after hour of impingements and demands. Encouragements, too, for sure. But for the most part, to become a serious tennis player, she was spending her developmental years being watched and corrected for hours each day. It struck me as a recipe for insecurity and narcissism.

"It's not much of a life, I guess, in terms of what we think of as childhood," Brian offered when I brought it up with him a little later. He was finishing his coffee at a picnic table between two courts, their green clay damp from the cloudbursts and squalls. I was stretching and eager to hit. "They don't have friends outside the academy, most of them," Brian went on to say. "And they aren't all that friendly with one another. I mean, they compete against each other. And they have these national rankings, and every kid they bump into at the tournaments they play at on weekends knows what the ranking is." He gestured with his chin to the court next to us, where a boy was rallying with an adult. "That's Preston. With his dad. Preston's twelve. Good forehand. You could learn watching that forehand—though the technique has been breaking down lately at tournaments. Ranked sixty nationally."

As we talked, Brian pushed back against some of the understandings I had about the kids who attend tennis academies. Much of what I knew, or thought I knew, I'd absorbed from Andre Agassi's *Open,* the best autobiography of a tennis player there is. Agassi, over his objections, had been sent by his father, at age thirteen, to Nick Bolletieri's now-legendary academy in Bradenton, on the west coast of Florida. He felt lonely, ostracized, abused, imprisoned. (Of course, he stayed, improved, and became a No. 1–ranked pro.)

"Here's the deal: These kids are here because they want to be here, most of them," Brian said. "I've had one or two kids whose parents were pushing them to do something they didn't want to do. But they don't last. These kids you see here are here because they love tennis—not every drill or every day, but they love tennis. They're athletes. Maybe the dad or mom is one, too. It's the life they know and the life they want."

"And what do they want, ultimately?"

"I honestly don't think these kids, the ones you see here now, think they're going to be top pros. You get realistic pretty fast. Your son is looking like he's going to be five-nine? Not going to cut it. But I think they'll play college, and some of them will get scholarships to do so."

The cost of attending the academy was $1,000 a week. (That's what I was paying.) If you wanted Macci's personal attention, that would cost you an extra $300 an hour. There were about forty young players currently enrolled at the academy, kids from around the country and also from Western Europe, Russia, and Asia. The families moved to a nearby condo and life revolved around the academy. Parents chose a particular academy depending on what other young players it was attracting; Macci's academy just then had a fair number of good young girls, which was making it attractive to parents with good girl players. That said, the Florida academies were not turning out top players as they did a generation ago. The United States was no longer a tennis power. Spain had become the place where the very best wanted to train, if training at an academy was part of the plan. For an increasing number of young prospects, working individually with a coach closer to home was now the way to go.

The boys and girls attending the Macci Academy were on the court at least four hours a day, five days a week. For four hours in the middle of the day, they got homeschooled. There could be hours in the gym each day, too, though Brian was not a proponent of gym time, unless a player was recovering from an injury that was keeping her or him off the court.

I asked him about Remi Ramos, the young player he worked with who was assisting him with his assessment technology and recovering from an injured hip that required surgery.

Brian bit his lower lip. "We're still working, a lot of it in the gym. And I sit her on a stool out here and work on her strokes. She's still got the strokes. You could learn from watching her."

He grabbed his iPhone off the table. "Here, look at this." He swiped a couple of times on the screen and there appeared a photo of a tiny girl clutching a racquet.

"She's four," he said. "From Jamaica. Her father says the courts there are so bad you can't play on them. So he taught her by looking at the videos on my website and then practicing phantom swings in their living room. Loves tennis. Kind of incredible, don't you think?"

He put the phone down and picked up his racquet, pounding the strings a few times with the palm of his hand. "Here's the deal: There is just no way to get really good without specializing early and putting in the hours with the right coach. There's not a top pro player or college player who hasn't done it. It's completely different from when you and I were kids, completely different. But the tennis is better, too. Those players you love to watch, you pay to watch? This is what it took to get that good."

I knew he was right, of course. The best tennis players in the world start early—on average, age six and a half. I'd happened upon *that* statistic while reading around in the research of the Swedish cognitive psychologist K. Anders Ericsson. Lots of writers have been delving into Ericsson since Malcolm Gladwell popularized his thinking in his book *Outliers*. Ericsson's Big Idea, in essence, is that world-class performers—in music, say, or chess, or tennis—are more made than born, and that the crucial ingredient is "deliberative practice": ten years or more of intense, individual instruction, beginning in early childhood, under the watchful eye of a serious coach or teacher and often spurred on by a demanding parent. Expert performers in tennis, for example, devote ten thousand hours to rigorously practicing only that, specializing rather than playing a number of organized sports and wasting no time goofing around on a tennis court with their friends. Such players are pretty much made by the time they are sixteen or seventeen.

Popularizers of Ericsson and their devotees (though not necessarily Ericsson himself) would seem to believe that the idea of the prodigy has been debunked. In an age that rewards those who study hard and test well with the help of prep courses, it's perhaps not hard to see why the ten-thousand-hours idea has been so readily embraced. But few I have met at the very top of tennis fully buy it. And they have more than anecdotal evidence to back them up. In 1978, a German psychologist named Wolfgang Schneider, with the help of the German Tennis Federation and a research team from the University of Heidelberg, recruited 106 of the most promising child tennis players from national juniors teams in Germany, all between the ages of eight and twelve. (Astonishingly, ninety-eight of these kids eventually played professional tennis and two of them became world-class champions: Boris Becker and Steffi Graf.) Schneider's study was designed to find out, because the German Tennis Federation was more than curious to know, whether greatness could be scientifically predicted—whether there was a way to foresee who was most likely to go on, in young adulthood, to be a top player. And, it turned out, there sort of was.

Each year for five straight years, Schneider and his researchers conducted two sets of tests on the young players. The first was designed to measure tennis-specific skills, the kind of skills acquired through what would come to be called deliberative practice: hitting targets with a serve or consistently returning forehands crosscourt. The second set of tests was to measure more general athleticism, and included a sprint and a start-and-stop agility test, along with psychological assessments of such things as competitive desire and physiological measurements of, for example, lung capacity.

Years later, the researchers took this data and set it alongside the professional rankings their lab subjects had achieved as adults. It turned out that scores on the tennis-specific part of the test predicted 60 to 70 percent of the variance in the adult rankings the children went on to achieve. The practice had mattered. Nurture was crucial. But the remaining 30 to 40 percent depended on a given player's athletic gifts. Without factoring in these gifts, the prediction model broke down. As Schneider would later tell the *Sports Illustrated* science writer David Epstein for his enlightening book, *The Sports Gene,* he and his researchers concluded that the children who were faster and more agile were, as a result of these gifts, significantly better at acquiring the tennis-specific skills that would make them the finer players. (They were *quicker* learners, for one thing.) And, keep in mind, these faster, more agile children were besting children who themselves were *athletes.* Imagine how their innate gifts would stack up against, say, a ten-year-old *me.* (Steffi Graf, by the way, outperformed, as a child, all the other children on tennis-specific tests *and* basic motor skills.)

People around tennis talk of players being born with speed and flexibility, which is not surprising, and having competitive desire from somewhere (or someone) by the time they begin taking childhood lessons. Increasingly, at the top levels of the game, height is a factor, and you can't teach height. (I have spent my life getting lessons in that.) And then there is visual acuity. By and large, great tennis players were born with great vision: 20/15, 20/10. That is, they see at twenty feet what a person with average vision sees only at fifteen or ten. And they also have keen depth perception. (Whether excellent depth perception is essentially innate or acquired is unclear, but astigmatism, which results in poor depth perception, is something you are born with, though it is correctible.) A 1986 study of U.S. Open tennis players found this to be true: They saw more, and more sharply, than non-players their age. And of course they had spent their learning years seeing much, much better than I could as I approached sixty.

It isn't that having keen visual acuity necessarily speeds up a person's reaction time, though having better-than-average depth perception can help when a ball is coming at you at a very high speed—a 135-mph serve, for example. Tests of professional athletes tend to show that their reaction time—one-fifth of a second—is essentially the same as that of an average person of the same age. What seeing very well provides is a tool for picking up anticipatory cues, "tells," as players call them. A great player with great eyes who has spent years practicing notices things I would have never noticed at any stage of my life, with however much practice—they pick up a ball's spin very early; they know in a quick scan that the way an opponent's hitting arm is cocked means the forehand about to be struck is headed crosscourt and not down the line.

And that player awaiting the forehand is not *thinking* about this. Bruce Abernethy, a human-movement researcher at the University of Queensland, has spent years studying athletes of all kinds. Among his findings is that elite tennis players, with their terrific eyesight, need less time than the rest of us to know what is coming at them from the other side of the net because they have "chunked" information about opponents' bodies and game situations—that is, they are not blurrily seeing and confronting lots of individual bits of information under pressure but intuiting familiar patterns finely perceived and then etched in their minds over years of practicing and playing. These chunks, once developed, are moved from a player's frontal lobe—where we do our conscious thinking—to the deeper recesses that control more automated processes. Abernethy found that top tennis players could anticipate where a serve was going by picking up not the ball's trajectory or even the motion of the racquet but by glimpsing tiny shifts in an opponent's torso early in the service motion.

The girl I had watched from my car as I finished my coffee, and the pre-K tennis whiz Brian showed me on his phone, going through her progressions in her Jamaican home: If these girls shared a goal to get to the very top, all the practice and determination in the world, all the thousands of hours, would not be enough to get them there. They might turn out to be too short, or too prone to injury, or too slow to pick up the ball with their average vision, or too well-adjusted to muster the drive to win.

Selfishly, the idea that a real tennis player is not just made but born comforted me. Short, skinny me would never have cut it. And, now, aging me didn't have ten thousand hours for tennis. I was at a point in life when I couldn't be certain I had ten thousand hours left for anything.

24

My routine at the academy during my days there was this: Each morning, from nine till eleven, I'd work with Brian on my forehand—"go through the progressions," as he would say. I'd then drive into downtown Boca, to a luncheonette I'd found in a strip mall, and eat lox and eggs and drink lots of iced coffee and read the papers. Then I'd drive back to the academy for two or three more hours of drills and instruction on other aspects of the game: serving, slicing, volleying. I'd then drive back to my motel room in Lauderdale-By-The-Sea, shower, walk to a seafood place for an early dinner, and be happily in bed by nine. If nothing else, I'd come to learn, spending hours training on a tennis court is a remarkable sleep aid.

I loved how seriously Brian took my strokes—he simply knew no other way of going about things. The key to the forehand, or *his* idea of the ideal forehand, was to have your hitting arm—before whipping it forward, toward the ball—extended out from the body, back and down, the arm straightened, the wrist laid back, and the racquet head up. This, let it be stated, is even more difficult than it sounds. Brian would start each morning on my side of the net with a hopper of balls, feeding them to me on the forehand side as I stood still with my racquet back, but also stopping more than occasionally to make micro-adjustments to my swing:

- "That Eastern grip of yours is too close to a Continental. Get under the racquet more. Slide it a tiny bit clockwise."
- "Can you get your arm a little straighter? Okay, if you can't. Del Potro is really the only guy who gets it really straight." (Juan del Potro, the Argentine pro, also hits forehands harder than any man alive. A few have been clocked at 120 mph.)
- "When you turn to take the racquet back, you want to feel just a little tug in the front shoulder. That's when you've turned enough. Feel it?"

I was understanding the mechanics of a forehand swing better, even if my forehand was not about to improve all that much. I was understanding how a promising ten-year-old could enjoy the coaching attention she was getting, though my attention was going to be for days, not years—and years of it I could not abide or have abided. But I was also understanding my body better: how and when certain muscles fired; where power came from, and didn't; and how your body resisted doing things you wanted it to do until you understood the way *your body* wanted to do them.

During one of our morning sessions, for example, the day already hot, the sky opalescent, Brian had me running for forehands across the full length of the baseline, corner to corner: twenty-seven feet. I would stand in the deuce corner; he'd hit a ball crisply from back behind his baseline to the ad corner; I'd split-step and take off for it. After the first three, he stopped and approached the net.

"If you are going to make this shot, you have to get to the ball in time to properly set up," he explained. "Your stance may be more open"—that is, my shoulder not turned—"and you may not have time to bring your racquet back so far, but shortening the swing is okay. But you have to be set up. And that means running with your racquet up and back. Not running with your racquet just in your hand and sprinting with it like a baton."

I tried running with my racquet up. I couldn't get to the ball. One, two, three times, Brian's shots passed me, clean winners. With my racquet up and ready, my speed dropped, I'd say, by as much as 20 percent.

Brian came to the net again. "I know it's hard," he said. "Your body does not want to move with the hands outside the torso. Interesting, isn't it? Your body is telling your mind that. It feels awkward. It's afraid of losing its balance. It thinks it knows something you don't."

I was mesmerized.

"But here's the deal: It's why you are late to the ball when it's a ball hit with pace. You have the quickness in your legs. That's not the problem. You have got to train yourself—train your body to overrule those signals it's getting. That preparation is something *you* can control. It has got to become automatic. By the time you position yourself to hit the ball, the only thing that should be left to do is swing and *whack*."

I took a water break and found myself thinking of my earliest lessons with Kirill, and how he kept urging me to take smaller steps as I approached the ball to more exactly position myself to hit it. The longish strides I'd taken on baseball fields and basketball courts were of next to no use in tennis. (It is not a coincidence that a number of the best modern-era tennis players—McEnroe and Federer among them—had been very good youth soccer players.) I was still pretty quick, but I would have to reengineer that quickness, starting with how I started. It was the knee bending, the getting down, that I was resisting at the start, and into my mind, during one of those early days with Kirill, floated an observation from one of John Updike's elegant golf essays about how we *feel* the strength of our straightened legs, tightened and tall, as we never quite do when we are crouched even slightly, so we keep straightening them exactly when we shouldn't. Bent knees are just counterintuitive—like short strides and shuffling sideways toward a tennis ball you're pursuing along the baseline rather than turning and sprinting toward it; and, for that matter, taking what's called a split step (elevating slightly, with a hop, one or two inches) as your opponent is about to hit a ball; and then, just after you hit a ball, taking that first step out and slightly sideways to begin shuffling again back to the middle of the court without even watching whether the ball you've just struck has cleared the net. All of this was, for me, worse than counterintuitive, actually. I simply could not tell if my legs were straight or bent, my strides long or short. I didn't know myself in that way.

And now, from Brian, I was learning that my torso wanted my arms close by when I ran. My week with Brian was filled with moments like this. I was not becoming an athlete, but my exposure to what that took for those who are athletes was introducing me to my body, or anyway, aspects of it—of how my body worked. An afternoon of volleying taught me that it was my pectoral muscles I needed to engage on my forehand volley, squeezing in with my chest; and it was my upper-back muscles, pinching them, that added pop to my backhand volleys. I wasn't leveraging fully the power to be drawn from my elbow as I made contact on my serve—wasn't snapping down on the ball. To get to a ball out wide on my backhand side, I was better off taking a couple of big shuffle steps toward it than running toward it: I'd get there faster (trust me; I tried it), and, with my shoulders squared to the net, be able to track the ball with both eyes rather than just my left, dashing with my head partially turned.

"It feels awkward," I found myself telling Brian more than once. And when I stopped to think about it, his suggestions often seemed illogical to me.

"We are always telling tennis players—telling ourselves—how to get the body to do things," he said at one point. "What I would say is that you have to learn—and it's not easy at your age—to let the body do it and then when you *feel* it, when you know *that's* right, find some language for it."

25

My last night in Florida I invited Brian to have dinner with me. We arranged to meet at the fresh-catch place I'd been eating at by myself with a book for company every night, a tiny restaurant called Sea, on a commercial strip running east-west, from I-95 to the ocean. I arrived first and took a table outside. It was on a stretch of sidewalk that looked out onto a parking lot, but I didn't mind. It was seventy degrees in January, and I drank cold white wine and watched clouds scud by a grapefruit moon suspended out there over the Atlantic.

Brian arrived in his tennis clothes. He'd finished his day at the gym, with Remi. "She wants to be a tennis player," he said, and left it at that. (And she would get to be one: After suffering a second hip injury, she recovered and went on to play for Boston University.) He sank into a chair, tugged off his tennis cap, scratched his head, and ordered a beer. His day had begun at dawn, he told me, with a bike ride along the beachfront up in Boca, where he rents a condo. "My exercise," he said, and grinned. His days were long, and he'd never really adjusted to the south Florida heat and humidity, and his wife just now was back in Indiana, to where he returned every few weeks. He loved tennis, he loved coaching, but what really interested him was the biomechanical research and theorizing he did on ground-stroke techniques.

"What I'd like to do is coach coaches," he said. "You have all these former players coaching, and there are things they know. But there are things they don't know, that *I* know. Things you can't just pick up on the tennis court." A thought passed: Brian, an athlete, if an aging one, was longing to live more in his head as I was longing to live less in mine.

He asked me if I'd recovered from the last drill he had me do, and smiled. I smiled, too, and shook my head. Late that afternoon, with the sun still high, he instructed me as follows: I was to start at the net with a volley. Then he would loft a ball behind me. If it was not too deep, set to fall inside the service line, I was to smash an overhead. If it drifted deeper, a lob, I was to run it down and return it. Then I was to rush back to the net to hit another volley, and continue the sequence. The goal was to hit fifteen straight balls over the net. And every time I missed, he deducted five from the total I'd accumulated to that point. It took me nearly twenty minutes of ragged running—cotton-mouthed, the sunscreen-laced sweat stinging my eyes—to finally reach fifteen.

"I really dug that drill in college," Brian said now, as we munched our salads. "Actually, I thought most drills were a good time."

And quickly enough, he was back there, replaying one match and then another for me. He explained that his was a serve-and-volley game, and that for a stretch of two college seasons, maybe, he never hit a groundstroke while he was serving. He recalled a match that began by his being unable to return his opponent's high and sharply angled kick serve—"missed a dozen of them"—but he adjusted and won. Listening, I thought of how easily those of us who aren't athletes and never were can hear in this kind of talk a certain sadness, Springsteen's "Glory Days," and also, as we absorb the stories in silence, feel affirmed in our life choices: studiousness, professional attainment, life of the mind. We would be wiser, I think, to consider that athletes know things—about fear, about adversity, about risk, about joy, about themselves, about life—that we never will.

When our fish arrived, I asked Brian what he thought about my game. He took his time before answering.

"You have wheels, you can move," he began. "Your strokes are all over the place. There are all these muscles that you are still not engaging, or engaging properly. And I'm not really sure what to do about that."

He told me he didn't know all that much about older players and what they could or could not learn. The senior players he coached from time to time were former Division I college athletes, men in their thirties and forties, who lived nearby and played tournaments and saw him for what amounted to tune-ups.

"What I'd say is that if your expectations aren't crazy, then what you are doing isn't crazy," he told me. "The part of me that looks at you biomechanically says, Look at this guy. He's probably engaging whole muscle groups he never engaged in his life. I'm helping him to engage more of them. Maximize them. And by doing that, engaging those muscles, you will improve your technique.

"Here's the deal: Improve your technique, you play better," Brian went on to conclude. "And the better you play, the more you will enjoy the game, right? I mean, at whatever age, what's so crazy about that?"

26

Kirill is an uncanny mimic—on-court mimic, I mean. The first time I hit with him, seeing I was a lefty, he served to me (with his right hand, being right-handed) a drop-dead version of southpaw John McEnroe's famous serve: feet planted wide and pointing away from the baseline; moon-launch ball toss; back turned to the net, soon to be deeply arched; the hitting arm sweeping wide to impart the patently severe slice. Kirill even followed his serve by ambling to the net, his racquet casually dangling, per Johnny Mac, ready to volley softly, deftly.

So it didn't surprise me that after I told him, right after my pounding at Forest Hills, that I wanted to spend the fall and winter learning a proper flat serve—a *real* serve, a first serve, a serve that might reach 85 mph, to complement my stolid, barely *serviceable* slice serve—he began my first lesson in that pursuit by demonstrating the serves of the world's top four men's players. I was to watch with a mind to choosing what type of service motion I wanted to have, or, anyway, to try to develop. He first did his Andy Murray, then his Rafael Nadal. Both employ what is known as a "pinpoint" serve: After tossing the ball, each slides his back foot toward the front one until the two nearly kiss. Murray's slide is longer than Nadal's, I was noting as I watched Kirill, and both make use of the pinpoint (as more women players seem to do today than men) because, the theory goes, with the feet forming a single, tight unit, the push-off puts more leg strength into the kinetic chain up to the arm, creating, ultimately, more arm speed and thus velocity.

"I don't think you want a pinpoint serve," Kirill gently suggested after a few Murrays and Nadals. By which he meant: *No way I am wasting a winter trying to teach you what you will never pick up.* He explained that the timing of a pinpoint serve is particularly intricate, with so many moving parts, and that because the feet, once drawn together, form a very small base of support, balance becomes a problem. My balance, though good for a man my age, was still, roughly, the balance of a sixty-year-old. I would neither be steady nor ready, up on my pinpoint toes.

"So what do Murray and Nadal do different?" Kirill went on to ask. I mentioned that Murray's slide was longer. "What else? Something more important than that." I'd watched him do each of their serves three times but had no idea. "Murray's tossing arm and hitting arm go up together, Rafa's don't. Watch closely. These things make a big difference in approach and timing."

Kirill now did his Federer and Djokovic. Both use what's called a "platform" serve. The feet are kept about shoulder-width apart throughout the serving motion, which provides stable support. There's a weight transfer from back foot to front during the racquet swing, the hips rotate, and the back foot swings forward to complete the hip rotation—not unlike when a pitcher throws a baseball. Djokovic (Kirill's imitation was spot-on) arches his back more deeply than Federer; and, watching more closely, as Kirill had urged, I picked up that

Djokovic began bending his knees as soon as he tossed the ball, while Federer paused till the ball was reaching its highest point, a yard or so above his head, before his knees bent down and forward toward the court, his back shoulder dropped, and he launched into his swing.

There was no way I was going to arch my back like Djokovic. Of course, there was no way I was ever going to serve like Federer, either. But Federer's approach to serving, as Kirill, explained it, would be the easiest for me to learn. "He is very fluid," Kirill said as he finished his demonstration. I sipped water and listened. "Will you get that fluid?" That was his way of saying, *You will not get that fluid.* Kirill, I had come to know, is very good at asking questions that contain their own answers.

I smiled, just a little wistfully.

He smiled, and tacked. "It can be broken down into parts, Federer's serve. And it will slow you down, Gerry. The way you rush things sometimes?" (Which is to say: *The way I almost always rush things.*) "The motion will help you to slow things down." He said, again, that it would be the easiest serving motion for me to do. He was careful not to say it would be easy, and it would not be. It would turn out to be about the hardest thing I've ever tried to learn. Which meant that if and when I *did* learn it, I would have a whole lot psychically and emotionally tied up with the accomplishment. It is one thing to confront the things you cannot do in your sixties. It's another to get the hang of something at that age—something difficult and by its very nature temperamental, which serving a tennis ball is. Can you count on it? Hold on to it? Make it a part of you in that way?

27

We humans tend to have a strong hand preference. We are alone among the primates, it seems, in being overwhelmingly handed (though monkeys and apes in captivity have been shown to develop handedness). Most of us—somewhere between 75 and 90 percent—are right-handed, and there is no certainty as to why. Somewhere between 10 and 15 percent of us are—like me—left-handed, and we are said to be over-represented in tennis, where our being "other-handed" has an advantage: We are used to righties, their angles and spins; they are not used to lefties. (A few of us—people, not tennis pros—are mixed-handed, doing some tasks with one hand, others with the other. True ambidexterity is rare.)

There is evidence for genetic influence in the determination of handedness; evidence that it is affected (and altered) by cultural and societal norms; evidence that it is connected to prenatal development processes, as the fetal brain develops distinct cerebral hemispheres. As the neurologist Frank R. Wilson suggests in his absorbing book *The Hand,* our hominid ancestors may have developed their handedness by throwing rocks at what they were hunting, realizing through trial and error that if they kept practicing with one arm and hand, they would throw more accurately. That seems plausible enough, though we cannot really know. Modern neuroscientific research has revealed that for almost all primates, voluntary sequential movements of the arms and hands are, in fact, executed with increasing fluency and precision the more they are repeated. My forehand attests to that, sort of. What I am absolutely certain of is that handedness has at least one drawback. It leaves us with a nondominant hand attached to a nondominant arm. And it's with this weak, slow, clumsy limb that a serve begins.

Holding a tennis ball out in front of you at thigh or waist height, rotating your shoulder joint in a natural, upward tossing motion, and releasing the ball to send it a few feet above your head would seem the easiest thing you might do on a tennis court. And you are standing still and in complete control, as you are not at any other moment in the unfolding of a tennis point. But when you are sixty, your nondominant arm has been doing a lot of nothing for a very long time. Your muscles are smaller and weaker than they are on your dominant side, your sense of control less. And then there is the whole challenge of quieting yourself, physically and mentally, in the midst of a game spent fiercely on the run. Even top pros can struggle with that.

The proper technique, or one of them—the one Kirill began to impart to me on the Har-Tru indoor court we had been spending our winters on for years—begins with holding the ball gently, like an egg, in a pincerlike grip, at the tips of your thumb and three fingers. Ideally, the ball should leave each of those digits at precisely the same time. What time? When your rising arm reaches the height of your eyes. Release it earlier and the ball could go anywhere—behind you, too far out in front of you, way to the left or right. Actually, it could do that at whatever height you release it at if your shoulder rotation follows its natural circular path. So you have to lock your elbow, firm and straighten your arm, and raise it out in front of you as if guiding the ball up a drainpipe. In sum, then, to execute a decent service toss, you have to be relaxed yet intensely focused, gentle-handed but rod-armed. The ability to confidently and fluidly and repeatedly carry out such divergent—but wholly purposeful—actions is to be an athlete, which I am not.

Serena Williams may be the greatest woman athlete to ever play a sport. She is certainly the greatest woman tennis player I've ever seen. One mizzly morning at Wimbledon some years ago, I stood with forty or fifty other fans alongside Court No. 15 and watched her practice her serve. She was wearing a loose T-shirt, and black calf-length tights that accentuated her imposingly muscular thighs. Without her ferocious game face on, I recognized, as I somehow never had before, her particular beauty—high cheekbones; wide-set eyes; big, relaxed smile.

The ryegrass was damp, so she would not be rallying with her hitting partner, as scheduled. Instead, Serena stood on the baseline and served and served again—the best serve in woman's tennis, and, according to some, like the coaching sage Nick Bollettieri, a smoother serving motion than any man. There is a way she has of not doing too much: not bending her knees too deeply, not transferring her weight back too extremely. Her power is generated by those thighs, that right arm and shoulder of hers (the racquet-head speed!), and her precise timing: Her way of knifing her racquet up on edge toward the ball and pronating at just the right moment is state-of-the-art for those of us who dream of serving hard. But when I think back to that half hour or so I spent watching Serena practice at Wimbledon, I think mostly about her toss. It's a marvel of technique and consistency. The long fingers of her left hand caress the ball—it nearly disappears without ever settling in her palm—and as her tossing arm rises from mid-thigh, it never bends, continuing its statuesque reach for the sky even after the ball has been released at eye level to ascend, on its own, a little farther. And the ball, soon enough, was always poised in the same spot up there, at the top of its trajectory, waiting high and still to be reached for and whacked flat or sliced with sidespin.

All that winter, before leaving the house on Saturday morning for my ninety minutes with Kirill, I would watch a forty-second, slow-motion YouTube video of Serena serving, and listen as Fred Stolle, the venerable tennis commentator and onetime Australian champ, remarks to Martina Navratilova—though you'll forgive me for thinking he was speaking directly to me, reminding me, exhorting me: "That left arm is so straight . . . not much can go wrong with *that* ball toss."

28

A tennis serve is over fast: in less than two seconds once you've begun the toss. But so much is going on in that time, and it all has to unfold sequentially and so precisely to result in a fine serve. And pretty much every one of those steps demands something of you that you have never done until you have served a tennis ball. Week after wintry week, on that musty indoor Har-Tru court in New Rochelle, Kirill took me patiently through those few seconds of movement and motion. He stood beside me, handing me balls, encouraging me, and, from time to time, adjusting my arms, my shoulders, my feet. There's an intimacy to imparting physical knowledge, to teaching an action—think of dance instructors—and the closeness is peculiar if you are student late in life. *This is what rehab after a hip replacement must feel like,* I thought to myself during one lesson, and got distracted.

I was struck, too, in these serving sessions, by how much I wanted to earn Kirill's approval. I wasn't needy in that way at home or at work, and never had been, for better and for worse. But here I was, seeking out eye contact with him whenever I managed to do something right—and dropping my gaze to the baseline when I hadn't.

- I practiced my toss . . .
- I practiced, once I'd released the toss: getting up on the balls of my feet, with my knees bent, my body turned sideways to the court, my right hip jutting toward the net and my knees in that direction, too, while at the same time shifting my weight to my back foot . . .
- I practiced, as my knees were bending: bringing my left arm, my hitting arm, up into the time-honored "trophy pose," my hitting shoulder dropped a bit; the arm at shoulder height; the elbow bent so the upper arm and lower arm form an L, à la Federer; and my racquet tilted forward about forty-five degrees . . .
- I practiced (once my knees were bent, I was up on the balls of my feet, and I'd gotten to the trophy pose): pausing; keeping my head up, eye on the ball; holding the racquet *loosely* with a Continental grip, not firmly with that grip, as I had learned to do when volleying. . . .
- My brief pause over, I practiced: dropping my racquet head down behind me, "scratching my back," and raising my body up and out toward the ball while beginning my swing up to meet the ball with a snap down on it before following through. . . .
- I practiced patience: I gained a whole new understanding that winter of "uncoordinated" and "chagrined."

Some weeks that winter I could not, for the life of me, get the toss to rise where I wanted it to—which was a foot inside the court, a foot to the left of my tossing shoulder, a yard or so above my head. Other weeks I was swinging too soon, or too late, or not getting my legs into it, or not sufficiently following through. On any given week, out of sixty serves or so, I might hit four or five that cracked—you can *hear* a good serve—and went in. After three months of serving lessons, Kirill had me simplify things by starting in the trophy pose, eliminating the step of bringing the racquet up in tandem with the ball toss. That helped my timing, except when it didn't.

And then one chilly Saturday in late February, almost four months after we had begun working on my service game, the serves just came, one after another, cracking. I hit some long and netted others, of course. But my timing was there and my ball strikes were clean. It all *felt* fluid for the first time. I cannot find the words for how good that felt. I was hitting a tennis ball harder than I ever had. And I was understanding—as I perhaps had never understood, really, before—that patience can pay off.

29

Back in the 1970s, an MIT graduate student in computer science and engineering named Howard Austin was awarded his doctoral degree for writing a mechanical analysis of the act of juggling—specifically, for challenging the notion, that I had embraced that February morning, that learning and mastering a motor skill happens gradually but steadily. Austin found, through his research, that jugglers tended to develop their skills episodically, with wild fluctuations of progress and setback, breakthrough and regress. While the overall direction was of gradual improvement over time, the climb was discontinuous. The sudden leaps in success were exhilarating to his jugglers—as mine that morning was for me. But what had brought about the breakthrough could not necessarily be understood and stored away for next time. Backsliding loomed.

I came to fully embrace Austin's conclusions soon enough. The week after my breakthrough, I was back to struggling in my lesson with Kirill. Still, I decided it was time to game-test my new serve. I arranged to play a match indoors on a nearby hard court with Shaun and introduce him to it. We'd been playing each other for a year or so by then, Shaun and I. He's eight, nine years younger than me, a big man with a strong upper body, an affable guy with an inquisitive streak that serves him well as a reporter for ESPN. Our matches could be sharp or ragged, depending, but I tended to win most of them, and win them the same way each time we played. Shaun has a long forehand swing and he likes to hit hard. My game was to take pace off the ball, with both my serve and my ground strokes, and let him generate his own pace with that big windup of his. His unforced errors would accumulate—balls heading to the back fence like missiles—and eventually he would commence the self-berating and racquet throwing: signs that the match was mine.

But on this particular afternoon, trotting out my new serve for the first time, I was the one who was soon enough berating himself. My old, flat-footed, low-toss spin serve to Shaun's backhand never produced an ace. But I got a lot of cheap service winners and easy enough put-aways (not that I converted even half of them) by placing my serve short in the deuce court, wide in the ad court, and forcing him to hit up. Now I was hitting a harder serve (85 mph on a good one, Kirill estimated) but a flatter one—and one I had no ability to place. I tossed and bent and trophy-posed and fired away, and, more often than not, the ball found its way to Shaun's forehand. And then back to me—and a few times right past me—before I'd gotten my feet set to get into the point. My new and better serve, so satisfying during my lessons with Kirill, had turned out to be a liability. It was crippling my game. I was sure there was some Zen life lesson in there. Mostly I was pissed.

It got worse. Being pissed on a tennis court always makes things worse. Connors, McEnroe: They weren't really pissed. They were shouting down their inner fears, intimidating their opponents, *using* anger, its dynamics, the way stressed-out hedge-fund managers use meditation. I was flat-out pissed: at myself and my crazy dream of having a real serve and Kirill for entertaining it and life for affording me health and drive just good enough at sixty to fail at tennis.

And now, having barely escaped the first set, 7–5, I was suddenly down 0–3, mostly because I had double-faulted two games away. My tosses were going every which way. I could feel the tension in my hitting arm and couldn't relax it. One after another of my serves fell a foot long or found the net. I could hear Kirill's voice, hear him telling me to step away from the baseline, take deep breaths, wiggle my fingers and shake my arm to relax. But I was drowning him out with my self-directed railings. I had never been a yeller on court, but here I was, head down, yelling in the direction of my tennis shoes:

> I *so* suck!
> You *so* suck!
> Gerry, how much do you suck?
> *You fucking suck so much!*

I won only two games in the second set. "I am feeling for you, dude," Shaun offered softly as we gulped water and toweled away the sweat before the third set. *I* was feeling for me. The double-faulting continued, the rest of my game sank to the level of my fugitive serve (as it will even for players much better than me), and Shaun—whose confidence and play naturally rose as mine reeled—took the third set 6–3 (which sounds closer than it was).

When I e-mailed Alexandra a few days later about my serving meltdown, she let me know that she was fascinated by the serving "yips," as tennis players call them. "There are *so* many fun psychological ways to come at describing what happens when a player steps up to the line, prepares to initiate the tennis conversation, and then finds himself jittery," she wrote.

"Or paralyzed with anxiety. Or is shut down by a sense of the inevitability of failure (or, worse, the possibility of success). Or discovers with horror that her mind has severed its ties—dis-*associated*—with her body."

She brought up James Hillman, the Jungian revivalist and New Age philosopher, and an essay he wrote on the half-boy, half-goat Greek demigod Pan. Their myths are our diseases, Jung famously said of the Greeks, and my "disease" at the baseline was panic. "According to Hillman," Alexandra explained, "anxiety and desire are the twin nuclei of the Pan archetype." I can't say I quite get everything Alexandra theorizes about the inner life in her Jungian way, but the idea that I would feel both desire and anxiety as I attempted to still myself and then attack a tennis ball—in the service of attacking my opponent—made perfect sense to me. (Alexandra: "What tennis player, as he pauses for an infinitesimal moment in the trophy pose, does not feel those dual nuclei alive in his core?")

Her therapeutic point? Her suggested cure for the yips? As the mythical Pan led men to battle with rituals, I needed rituals at the baseline in those moments before I started my service motion. I needed things like Nadal's curling his hair behind his ear and pulling at the back of his shorts; or Djokovic's bouncing the ball the same number of times before each serve. I needed an act that acknowledged my anxiety (the acknowledgment would itself calm me a bit), and that allowed me to channel whatever energy was generated by that anxiety into my desired gesture: successfully serving the ball.

I began looking off to my left, into the distance, as I assumed my platform stance at the baseline. I began taking a deep breath before bending to begin, then bouncing the ball precisely three times. And, in the beginning at least, feeling all this had become *way* too important to me.

30

I got a little obsessive about the serving. I would drive down to the club and hit serves against the wall on mornings before work when the temperature was barely above freezing. Some mornings there was a little snow beneath my sneakers. I'd hit wearing a fleece jacket, a watch cap, and gloves. I would pause in the trophy pose and catch myself feeling ridiculous. I would then tell myself I needed to work harder on my focus.

The truth is, I was happy—with the challenge, the determination I was mustering, the signs of improvement. Serving is the lone aspect of tennis you can practice on your own (unless you count having a machine feed balls to you). I liked that I was getting to try to work this out with no one watching. I'd hit a hundred serves, sometimes more—hit until my shoulder got too sore to swing.

I abandoned starting my serve in the trophy pose and went back to a full motion. I looked to the distance, breathed deeply, gave the ball three bounces on the cold, snow-patched concrete. And, in time, after weeks of practicing, it worked. Or, anyway, worked most of the time, *just* most of the time: 60, 65 percent of my first serves in the imaginary games I constructed for myself.

Not till I was ready, at the beginning of March, did I come to a lesson and show all this to Kirill. He did not disapprove (though who knows how strange he found the whole thing). After I'd drilled a few good ones, he took out his iPhone and digitally taped me with his Dartfish app. (Dartfish, too, had gone 2.0.) And when he captured one he liked, he beckoned me to have a look. I couldn't quite believe it. Yes, I looked just as old as I had in southern Utah at Green Valley. But I was *moving* and *flowing*. At the point I was contacting the ball, my feet were several inches off the ground! I asked Kirill to show me video one more time.

"Honestly, Gerry," he said. He was watching with me, and his hand was on my shoulder. "The toss is still too close to you—you want to be able to extend farther, out in front. And you are not pausing quite long enough, so that's why your contact is above the sweet spot. And you want more downward snap on contact. But honestly, that's not bad.

"Also, remember the big picture here," he went on to say. "You took a step backward to take a step forward. You gave up a serve that you got in much of the time and started over, from the beginning, on a real serve. Very few people at any level of tennis are willing to do that—even though that is the thing you have to do to improve in tennis. Always."

He held out his hand and we shook on that, firmly.

31

I spotted Alexandra: She was in a long, summery skirt and wearing a big hat against the desert sun, still so searing even as it neared its descent behind the distant mountains. It was the middle of the second week of the BNP Paribas Open, or Indian Wells, as fans call it, Indian Wells being the town, a half-hour drive south of Palm Springs, where the tournament is held each March. We'd arranged to meet outside the main entrance to Stadium 1, an immense arena, second in size only to Arthur Ashe at the U.S. Open in New York, but we knew we would have no problem finding each other. A busy afternoon at Indian Wells meant twenty thousand people or so spread around the roomy tennis-garden grounds at one or another of the three stadiums or many side courts or food courts or carefully tended, tree-shaded or tented oases. It was known as the "fifth slam" because almost all the top players played, because the winners' purses were substantial, and because Larry Ellison, the Oracle cofounder who owned and ran the tournament, had used his money and acumen to improve nearly every aspect of attending and experiencing a big-time sporting event, from parking to eating to viewing. It felt like a state fair with tennis where the animal judging should be. I'd penciled in Indian Wells as a winter-vacation destination, sometimes with Barbara (her oldest brother lived in L.A., and we'd visit) and other times, when she couldn't make it, as it turned out this year (she was in Havana with a group of her students), alone. Alone was always okay with me when it came to watching tennis, though I was looking forward to seeing Alexandra.

She's built like a Central European tennis player, big hipped and not tall, I'd thought when I first glimpsed her in Oakland, where we'd met for dinner nearly a year before. She had, it turned out, played high-school tennis, in a small town in upstate New York near Rochester. She'd come west after college to study at the C. G. Jung Institute in San Francisco, and still worked there; she was soon explaining to me, as we got ourselves a couple of lemonades and found a shady picnic table, how those responsibilities at the institute, along with her growing practice in Oakland, which she loved, were cutting into her blogging time. She was not, anyway, at Indian Wells to write about the matches but because she was working with a pair of double players. She could not, she told me, reveal exactly who they were, or what the issues were, and I didn't really need to know which player's or players' inner life she was helping to bring round.

She told me instead about her vacation trip to Melbourne and the Australian Open in January. Alexandra has a dark-eyed alertness and an easy smile that rises frequently to her high cheekbones, and the smile barely left her face as she told me, in her soft but not hesitant voice, about how Australians find a way to abbreviate every word they can: "Chocolate, you know, is 'choco' or sometimes just 'choc.'" She is attentive to language—"it was *the* tennis there; 'we're going to *the* tennis,' 'how was *the* tennis'"—and even more attentive to what goes on during a tennis match: She's a noticer. She told me about an early round match in Melbourne in which the Latvian Ernests Gulbis, maybe one of the surliest players on the men's tour, had, in the midst of an awful match he would lose to the American Sam Querrey, tossed his racquet down hard and vaguely in the direction of a ball kid. The racquet head smashed in half, and as Gulbis went to his chair at the side of the court to fetch and unwrap a fresh racquet, "he gestured to the child—not to apologize or anything but, in that Ernests way, to retrieve his vibration dampener from the piece of broken racquet head!"

As it happened, I'd had my own Ernests sighting two days before—he'd barked at a ball girl for not getting his towel to him quickly enough, giving rise to a loud chorus of boos from the crowd in cozy Stadium 3. He was playing a ragged third-round match he'd eventually win 2–6, 6–1, 7–5 against the young Bulgarian Grigor Dimitrov, who at twenty-two seemed to be coming into his own and—what drew me to the match—could be the last of a dying breed: a top pro who swings a one-handed backhand drive. I'd just begun working pretty intensely with Kirill on my one-hander, adding a ninety-minute private session on Sundays to the one I had on Saturday in an attempt to increase my topspin and improve my consistency from the backhand wing. I had made it my point in the few days I was spending at Indian Wells to watch as many players with one-handers as I could, not for instruction (God knows) but for inspiration, confidence, the *desire* to keep working on a shot I wanted so badly to hit and hit well.

Alexandra and I wandered off to a side court where I might get another dose of those things.

I talked to her on the way about a book I was reading, a short book by Hans Ulrich Gumbrecht, a German-born literature professor at Stanford, a book long forgotten, I imagined, and one steeped in Kantian seriousness, called *In Praise of Athletic Beauty*. It's a thought-inspiring essay in defense of being a sports fan. Gumbrecht admits to being a little defensive among his academic friends about his passion for sports; a little defensive, too, about finding so many moments of aesthetic marvel when he (writing as a man in his fifties) attends the home games of the Stanford Cardinal football team he loves. There is—there has been for years now—a defensiveness about finding and praising beauty even where it was once deemed most appropriate: in art galleries, say. The culture, or anyway those who create it and comment on it, have grown more interested in irony and transgression. Or, as Susan Sontag wrote in an essay on beauty she published a few years before Gumbrecht's book, what we're interested in now is not beauty but *interestingness*.

Alexandra and I were speculating about this kind of stuff as we settled in to watch Roger Federer practice on Court 7. (Gumbrecht has a nice riff about Federer: "We associate elegance and effortlessness with his flowing movements on the court that never seem to be centered on just one play.") One of the things I love about Indian Wells is that there is an electronic sign out by the practice courts that informs you which players are practicing where and when. Federer and Nadal, too, often practice at this tournament not on the practice courts, where there is mostly standing room, but on those courts where there is room for hundreds of fans to sit and watch greatness being honed and, alas, nowadays, hold up their phones and squeeze away, instantly thrilling their friends with ill-framed shots of far-off tennis stars. Our conversation drifted to my backhand, and hers—Alexandra told me she was playing more again and working with a teaching pro on *her* one-hander. She did suppose that *my* problem with *my* backhand (and maybe not only my backhand) had something to do with an inability to relax and free myself up. It's that long, uncoiling, arms-extended-like-a-ballerina-in-second-position openness that makes the one-hander so beautiful, we were telling each other. "Let *go*," she advised.

Federer arrived, in a gray T-shirt and black shorts, to applause, and began letting go again and again. At one point he hit thirty, forty backhands in a row, and I concentrated on how, with shuffle steps of the kind Brian Gordon had instructed me to take, he got to balls and then, executing a smooth shoulder turn, positioned and settled himself before swinging. We were right behind him, seven or eight rows up, sitting on the stairs—every seat in the stadium was already taken when we arrived. This is what real fans did: watched practice.

The previous afternoon I'd watched two matches from a near-nosebleed seat in the cavernous Stadium 1, concentrating on the magnificent backhand of Stan Wawrinka, whose sluggishness and poor serving cost him in a loss to South Africa's Kevin Anderson, and then those one-handers of Tommy Haas and Federer (a match Fed won efficiently, 6–4, 6–4). But I was mostly too far away to see the little things I was looking for—though I was wonder-struck more than once by Wawrinka's ability on the backhand wing to get on top of balls (for topspin) up near his shoulder (what strength! It brought his feet off the court!); and was delighted to hear (I'd been alerted to listen for this by Brian Gordon down in Boca) the distinct, deep-boom *sound* of Haas's backhand when he struck it just right.

Along with my distance from the court, high up and behind a baseline, I was dealing with, or not, the late-afternoon sun lasering my eyes and, worse, the incessant distractions of the casual fans around me: the drink fetching and sunscreen spraying, the texting and selfie taking. "Did someone win?" a young woman in the seat in front of me asked her boyfriend, as the crowd roared its approval of a high, backhand, putaway volley Fed had conjured. I'd become, in truth, a bit of a snob about things that had the potential to move me by being superbly or sublimely beautiful: the written word (foremost), paintings, films (foreign, mostly), tennis. And it was getting worse, my loftiness and disdainfulness, the older I got. Not that I acted in ways that others would notice. I kept my thoughts to myself. Another thing about aging, at least for me: I no longer care about *persuading* anyone.

Watching Fed practice, we were all snobs, or so I had persuaded myself. I was comfortable, despite my cement seat; content, attuned. There were long stretches of silent watching—that fluidity and consistency, the lovely ease of it all—and when he'd pause to towel off or sip some water (it was hot out there), the fans around Alexandra and me would chat knowledgeably and engagingly about Federer's new coach (the Swedish great of the late '80s and early '90s, Stefan Edberg) and his new racquet (with a larger head, and stylishly black). And then, when Fed resumed his hitting, all went quiet again, save for that certain thwock of a ball coming off the strings at the (now larger) racquet head's sweet spot. To disconnect from everyday life and then "to be lost in focused intensity": That, Gumbrecht wrote, opened us to the beauty to be found in sports, the "epiphanies of form" that "we have no right to expect" and so enthrall us all the more. Enthrall some of us, anyway.

32

The Plaza Racquet Club, situated amid the blocks of low-slung Spanish-mission-style homes just east of Palm Springs's main shopping streets, is the sweetest tennis club I know. It's not much to see, just nine well-maintained hard courts and a little tennis shop with a cement patio shaded by palms and dwarf trees. But there are Instagram-worthy views of the mountains from whichever baseline you are poised to serve, and the club's proprietors, Kurt and Ana Haggstrom, are the kind of people who keep you coming back to your favorite wine shop or neighborhood bistro. I come back to Plaza Racquet to play whenever I fly west to watch tennis at Indian Wells, and one of the things the Haggstroms will do is arrange matches for you if you call ahead and give them a week.

The courts are at their busiest in the morning, when it is still on the cool side and before the sun makes its way to where it blinds your service toss. And they are especially busy in the winter months, high season in Palm Springs. Not surprisingly, many of the players are retirees, and I have played numerous doubles matches with men (and a few women, too) who represent the end of an era—folks in their late fifties or early sixties living on defined pension plans, having retired from their jobs at Allstate or General Mills after twenty-five or thirty years and sold their suburban homes outside Chicago or Minneapolis (those I've met are largely transplanted Midwesterners) and downsized to a low-tax, low-maintenance place in one of the gated developments that sprawl to the city's south toward Palm Desert and Rancho Mirage. These retirees tend to stay in or around Palm Springs for eight, nine months, then escape to Maine or the mountains of North Carolina during the summer, when daytime temperatures in the desert average above one hundred degrees. They are set financially, fit, and engaged, at least on the tennis court, though I really can't attest to the state of their inner lives.

I can say that these retirees are not simply imprisoned in an oldster's penal colony, at least when they come to play tennis. Plaza Racquet has a considerable gay and lesbian membership. In fact, the club was home to the first USTA same-gender-spouses' tournament. Moreover, in March, when the Paribas Open is under way, there are dozens of guests from all over on the courts, guys like me paying $20 for court time, looking for a couple of hours of play before driving off to watch the pros. (The club's initiation fee, by the way, is all of $150, and annual membership is $550.)

On the last morning of my little tennis vacation, before I drove back to L.A. to catch my flight home, I played a singles match at Plaza Racquet. My opponent, introduced to me by Kurt Haggstrom, was a guest like me—Bill, tall and wide-shouldered, in his mid-fifties, with a thick coating of sunblock on his face and a wide-brimmed straw hat protecting his head. He was from Hawaii, where he ran a very successful roofing business, he told me as we made our way to our court. He'd grown up in Southern California, where he played tennis for his high-school team, and he and his wife liked to spend a week each winter in Palm Springs, especially now that their two kids were out of college and on into their own lives.

Like me, he was making a lot of time for tennis. He too had a USTA rating of 4.0—which, according to USTA guidelines, means you are someone who has "dependable" strokes, can handle "moderately" paced balls from both wings, and can "occasionally" force errors with your serve. The ratings run from 1.5 (a beginner) to 7.0 (a world-class player). These ratings are mushy, more or less self-enforced, and don't take age into account (I cannot hope to beat a twenty-five-year-old 4.0 player, but I do hope, when I enter national tournaments like the one at Forest Hills, to stay on the court with 5.0 players who are in their sixties.) My favorite sentence in the USTA's 4.0 guidelines, because it shows the impressionistic nature of the rankings and yet totally nails my game: "Rallies may be lost due to impatience."

I was being patient in the early going with Bill, holding my serve and feeling him out, and he was doing the same. He hit harder than me (no surprise) and I moved better than he did (no surprise there either). I was relaxed, and could sense my muscles and joints loosening as the desert morning warmed. We were tied at three games apiece, with me serving at 40–30 in game seven, when I struck a sharp-angled forehand that put Bill on the run to his backhand side. Realizing instantly (or sort of instantly) that a defensive slice would be his only option, I rushed (or sort of rushed) the net. He completely botched his backhand, knifing the ball down, where it landed three or four feet in front of him. Game mine.

During the changeover, at a courtside, canopied bench, Bill chuckled an anxious chuckle and offered, "Always lose it when somebody comes in." What was I supposed to do with *this*? In all the time I'd been playing, no opponent had ever come out and flatly stated his weakness. It's one thing to come to understand an opponent's strengths and weaknesses in the course of playing, and keep away from the former, if possible, while trying to exploit the latter. But here Bill was, *telling* me that he panics when you crash the net on him. What was going on? Was this, consciously or not, meant to make me uncomfortable about coming in? Make it seem unsportsman-like? After all, he'd just been so open, so honest—he'd owed up to a vulnerability. Was he messing with my head? He *was,* I'd decided by the time we headed back onto the court. Of course, deciding that gave me permission to exploit his weakness, and exploit it I did. It was only later that I thought to think I'd been unkind.

His first serve was long, and I moved in on his slower second serve, chipped it, and charged. He blasted a short fore-hand into the net. What followed was more, much more, of the same. I broke him and took that game, then held and won the next one, too, closing out the set, 6–3. And, in the second set, I kept coming in whenever the opportunity presented it-self, and even, at times, when it didn't. I hit drop shots and followed them toward the net; I served and volleyed. Bill's reaction to the sight of me nearing the net was nearly always the same, and increased in intensity as the set went on, and I kept winning: He'd hit the ball as hard as he could, as if he wanted to drive it right through me, and then glare and mutter obscenities to himself as the ball sailed long or wide or buried itself in the bottom of the net. And when he did manage to hit a ball in with me at the net, my volleys were pretty terrific: That's what confidence can do.

Bill was no longer speaking to me during the changeovers.

And me? I was, if I'm honest with myself, *loving* it. Not the tennis, exactly. No, worse: the merciless imposing of my will.

It was as if I was under some spell. But of course I wasn't. I was just acquainting myself with a part of my psyche I hadn't met before, or, anyway, had never so fondly engaged with. Tennis, which had already revealed so much of me to me, was showing me my desire to vanquish and a capacity for cruelty. I was torturing a guy—a stranger, someone I was unlikely to ever meet again, which probably made it easier—and having fun. The second set and thus the match was soon enough mine: 6–0.

"That wasn't much tennis," Bill said with a tight smile as we shook hands at the net. At the time I took that to mean the quality of *his* tennis. I shrugged and patted his back a couple of times.

33 |

Bob—Bob Litwin, the great senior player, onetime tennis coach and longtime life coach I'd met back in September—was trying, one, drear-drizzly morning in early May, to get me to understand my "old" story. By that he meant the current story of my inner state as a player, the one keeping me from playing better tennis (maybe), and even being a better person (perhaps), at least on court. To understand that story I had to first know what it was—had to explore my tennis persona, listen to the words I chose when describing my on-court self.

I was in a dark suit at my desk in my office on the sixteenth floor of the Times Building. Bob, in a T-shirt, was in his home office on Long Island. It was 8 a.m., and through the wonders of Skype I was having my biweekly counseling session with Bob. It was my sixty-first birthday present to myself. I was going to work to improve my mental game. Bob—as his coaching technique promised—was going to coax from me a new and better story of my tennis-playing self.

It has long been understood that the game of tennis has an outsize psychological dimension. Even those who didn't play the game came to understand that in the 1970s, when W. Timothy Gallwey published his *The Inner Game of Tennis* and soon found himself talking not only to athletes but to New Age seekers and business leaders. (Gallwey, you could say, invented the kind of life-coaching Bob does.) A tennis court—a space you enter to face someone whose aim is to defeat you—is a breeding ground for anger and fear, though I had never felt much of either (or so I had been telling myself). But I had felt impatience, frustration, anxiety, a lack of focus, and, in Palm Springs six weeks earlier, an animal urge to ride a man down—feelings you, of course, encounter often enough in day-to-day living, but which can arrive in strikingly (and sometimes cripplingly) concentrated form in the midst of a tennis match.

I was telling Bob this particular morning about a match I had played a few days earlier, a singles match—"third" singles, which is to say a matchup of third-best (of three) singles players in team tennis. I had joined a Sunday-afternoon team at my club, a team made up of 3.5- and 4.0-USTA-level players of various ages (though no one else playing singles was as old as me). I knew some of my teammates, but wasn't particularly close to any of them. It surprised me how much I found myself looking forward to the match and feeling part of a team—putting on my team polo; rooting for my teammates and being encouraged by them; having a beer together, when all the tennis was done, in the quieting that arrives with late Sunday afternoon. Being a team member—as an adult amateur—occupies a very particular emotional space: You're not friends or colleagues. You have lives that don't revolve around playing sports (you aren't really athletes). And at least in singles tennis, you are not actually playing *with* your teammates. You bond with one another over a series of matches unfolding on adjacent courts, for a short period of time outside of time. But you do compete to win, and you do learn things about your teammates—though tennis being tennis, you learn mostly about yourself.

The match I was talking to Bob about had taken place in nearby Scarsdale, at a lovely little club called Fox Hollow, and driving over I was in a mood as bright as the day: It would be my first match with the team, and the first time I'd played a match outdoors in Westchester in six months. My opponent and I soon found each other and introduced ourselves on the deck of the club's tennis house, which overlooked a half-dozen Har-Tru courts. His name was Glenn; he was tall, well-built, and a few years younger than me; he'd played on his high-school team on Long Island and then intramurals at Cornell, and for several years had been club champ at a country club in Scarsdale; he was a cardiologist and medical researcher affiliated with a couple of prestigious hospitals in New York. I immediately liked him, I told Bob, and could have talked with him for hours.

We were on the court soon enough, where two challenges immediately presented themselves. He was a lefty, like me, and I seldom played lefties. But as the match began I adjusted to that—I came to understand quickly enough that his backhand was not where I normally find an opponent's backhand, and that his slice serve would spin not into my body in the ad court, as a righty's does, but out wide on my forehand. I was settling into the match, and we were tied at three games apiece in the first set. But out of nowhere, I was telling Bob now, the wind suddenly picked up, gusting unpredictably and blowing what seemed like every which way. I could not adjust my service toss, a toss that had grown higher indoors over the winter, as Kirill and I worked on adding pace to my serve.

"When I lowered it, I netted my serves," I said, looking at Bob on my desktop screen. "When I took something off a serve to simply get it in, he crushed it. He went on to break me four times in the match, three times in long deuce games. I double-faulted like crazy—twice to lose games." Glenn had no problem simply lowering his already rather low toss. He beat me 6–3, 6–2.

Bob took a long sip of coffee out of his mug. Then he leaned forward, his face almost filling my desktop monitor: "So where was the wind when you were serving and staying in those long deuce games? You had to be winning those points, right? So your serve had to be okay, right?" He paused and looked away, letting that sink in. Silences when you are Skyping loom weirdly. I got what he was saying and smiled, goofily, at my bookcases.

"You talked about the wind, and you talked about your opponent's serve, his adjustments, and you told me the results of the match—that you lost," Bob went on to say. "That is the story you chose, the words you chose, to describe the match."

Another sip of coffee, another pause.

"Wind, bad conditions, tough afternoon to play—that's not part of a good story. Your opponent's ability to adjust— that's . . . Well, you tend to spend too much time discussing your opponent whenever we talk about your game, and we'll get back to that. Your serve: It seems to me that in certain big moments, pressure moments, you double-faulted. Maybe you lost confidence or focus. You felt nerves. You'd been working to improve your serve all winter, you'd told me when we began our first session. And now, in big points, in a match and not simply practicing with your coach, you didn't nail your serve."

One more pause. Bob was scribbling something down.

Then: "What I would like you to do, Gerry, is really dig deeper into yourself. I want you to begin writing down the elements that make up the old story of you, you and your tennis game. Maybe you need to ask yourself: Is part of my old story that I lose focus in big points? Or confidence? Lots of players do. And then I want to work with you to start writing a new story. What I hope that new story is going to do for you is get you to a place where on a windy day, serving at deuce in a tight match, you are saying to yourself, and mean it: 'We're in tennis heaven!'"

34

"You don't get to choose your opponents in tennis—
tournament tennis, team tennis," Bob was saying. It was
two weeks later, another Skype session first thing in the morning. A smile was broadening across his face, and he was slowly
shaking his head. "Right? You understand that. You have to.
But my bigger point to you would be: You should not be
thinking you are playing an opponent when you are playing
a match. You are playing a game. And, more specifically, you
are playing points. Part of your old story is: 'I think too much
about opponents.' And what we have to make part of your new
story is: 'I focus on points.'"

We were back at work, excavating my old story. We had
identified a couple elements of it. One was that I had not yet
come to terms with competition, how I felt about it. I knew
I loved learning and practicing. But competing? Another was
that I was impatient in a point and in a match. I was impatient
in life, too, of course. I had always *counted* on my impatience
to get me what I wanted. Impatience was my trusted ally. But it
wasn't working for me in tennis. I couldn't stay in the moment,
relax, remain focused.

I was telling Bob about a club singles tournament I

had entered the previous weekend. I'd won my first-round match, against a decent thirty-something player, in a grueling three-setter that ended in a long tiebreak, 12–10. On Sunday morning, in the second round, I'd faced a familiar opponent, Andrew, a fastidious and quietly fierce competitor six or seven years younger than me whose game, a good game, had long been driving me nuts. It's a game built around blocking your shots back with sliced underspin from both wings and hitting a lot of deep, high-arcing balls with little pace—moonballing, as it's known. It's the game of a "pusher" or "backboarder," a game meant to try and break your patience, a quality I have little of to begin with (see above). And Andrew has a way of enhancing the overall effect by taking an excruciatingly long time before serving and on changeovers: toweling, sipping water, wiping his glasses. . . . There are strategies suggested for countering this sort of game: coming to the net more, bringing the moonballer to the net, moonballing yourself. But these things are easier said than done, especially when your opponent has legs that get him to most balls and has been playing his game, refining it, since high school, as Andrew has.

I got up a break in each of the sets we played that morning. But then came the inevitable: I lost patience and began going for big, low-percentage shots. All the standing and waiting for balls to come down and bounce into my hitting zone not only messed up my timing; it somewhat paradoxically made my legs tired. You come to know, playing tennis, that fatigue has a lot to do with your mental state. If your mind is wandering, you're not signaling your knees to bend or your feet to get up on those toes: The bounce in your legs wanders away, too. Frustration gets you gripping your racquet too tightly, which makes your arm heavy. If you are feeling no rush of excitement, you get no adrenaline release.

I wind up hating my body in situations like that. And hating tennis, too—something I never feel during a trying session with Kirill, or when I am getting crushed by an opponent playing a faster, harder-paced game. I was feeling trapped by Andrew, coerced and confined by his game, and wanted out. I got my wish soon enough. He beat me 6–4, 6–3.

Bob had been taking notes while I relayed all this to him, and after pausing and looking over what he'd scribbled down, he lifted his head and that soft smile of his filled my desktop.

"There are a few things I am hearing," he began. "One is: 'I can't adapt.' That's a bad story. We are going to have to work on that."

I laughed a little.

"Another is—well, it's what I didn't hear. What did you learn in that match, Gerry? About yourself and your game? You are a learner, right? You took up tennis at the age you did to learn, to grow, to defy your age, perhaps. There was a learning experience in that match. I want you to be someone who learns every day. If you learn something every time you play, you will play better. And if you play better, you are likely to win more. That's how you grow. And growing is what playing is about, ultimately, or should be."

I was at the moment that comes when I talk with Bob that I see all the irony I am capable of sensing—and all the distancing it can afford me—kicking in. But it doesn't! I'm totally with him! I'm nodding and smiling. I understand now how people follow gurus to miserable jungle compounds.

"One more thing," he is saying now. "There *is* something special about finding that person or those people you love playing with. I get that. There's nothing wrong with feeling that. There are these guys I have been playing with for thirty years, and that's important to me. It's about those people who bring out the best in you as a player and a person. It's about relationships. I had this conversation once with Billie Jean King and she told me: 'Don't forget to tell your students it's not about the winning. You don't remember the winning so much. The trophy goes in the basement. What tennis can give you is those special relationships.'"

I jumped off our Skype connection and e-mailed Paul to see if he could play come Saturday.

35

Bob had gone off to play a tournament, and left me with instructions to spend the next couple of weeks drafting my old story. "Don't be afraid to put some emotion into it," he said. "The *why* isn't important. Just tell the story of you as it is today in this one area of life: tennis." He had e-mailed me a few samples written by young athletes he was working with, life-coaching. There was one by a squash player, not yet in high school, nationally ranked—already working through his old story! It was a litany of flaws and weaknesses: He let people's opinions of him affect him; he prejudged opponents; he played scared; he was nervous, afraid to lose, stubborn, unfocused, making excuses, not giving his all. I wondered if what he needed was just to get under the headphones with some loud music, like every other self-doubting (and thus self-loathing) thirteen-year-old I've ever known. I also wondered if his old story wasn't the old story of anyone who stepped onto a court or field or course at whatever age and set in motion the possibility of failure and loss. Really, what *are* we—what *am* I—doing out there?

It took me a week of evenings to draft my old story. I tried to be honest and specific. I fussed with it, fearing it was too fussy. Then I reached a point at which I thought: I can't be someone spending this much time polishing the presentation of his tennis shortcomings. I attached it to an e-mail and sent it to Bob:

- I don't know how I feel about competition, which makes me anxious.
- I'm impatient: I go for too much too often. I want to get on with things. I won't allow rallies to develop slowly. I can't stay in the moment.
- I see the match too much in terms of games, sets. I don't play points.
- I don't like thrashing opponents. I'm not comfortable with that. Do I want too much to be thought of as a nice guy?
- I lose focus, especially when I go up 30–0, 40–15. I don't finish. I only really focus in tight spots. I'm at my best serving down 4–5. Cold-blooded. Why can't I be that way up 5–2?
- I abandon shots quickly if they aren't working for me. I net two volleys, I stop coming in. I spray two inside-out forehands, I'm crosscourt only the rest of the match. I can't think: It'll come, relax.
- I can't let go of points an opponent wins on a badly struck shot. Win a lucky point from me with a mis-hit return, you probably win the next point, too.
- I am better battling not to lose than going for a win. Why can't I play up a set and a break like I play down a break in the third set?

I got an e-mail back from Bob a day later. He was working his way through the draw of his sixty-five-and-over clay-court tournament. He attached his edit of my old story.

- ~~I don't know how I feel about competition, which makes me anxious.~~
  My purpose/mission is unclear.

- ~~I'm impatient. I go for too much too often. I want to get on with things. I won't allow rallies to develop slowly. I can't stay in the moment.~~
  I'm impatient. Can't focus.

- ~~I see the match too much in terms of games, sets. I don't play points.~~
  I think too much about results.

- ~~I don't like thrashing opponents. I'm not comfortable with that. Do I want too much to be thought of as a nice guy?~~
  I want my opponents to like me.

- ~~I lose focus, especially when I go up 30–0, 40–15. I don't finish. I only really focus in tight spots. I'm at my best serving down 4–5. Cold blooded. Why can't I be that way up 5–2?~~
  I mentally multitask.

- ~~I abandon shots quickly if they aren't working for me. I net two volleys, I stop coming in. I spray two inside out forehands, I'm crosscourt only the rest of the match. I can't think: It'll come, relax.~~
  I am pessimistic. I don't follow through on my commitments.

- ~~I can't let go of points an opponent wins on a badly struck shot. Win a lucky point from me with a mis-hit~~

~~return, you probably win the next point, too.~~
I can't let go of the past.

- ~~I am better battling not to lose than going for a win.~~
  ~~Why can't I play up a set and a break like I play down~~
  ~~a break in the third set?~~
  I play not to lose.

I tried telling myself that I had to admire the bold starkness of Bob's editing, having been an editor myself for thirty-five years. That was my first reaction—perhaps, you know, because I wanted my opponents to like me. In truth, I felt unsettled, badly judged, defensive, *oppositional.* I didn't like the self that Bob had chiseled from my old story, and worried that the implication was that this was who I really was not only on a tennis court but outside the lines, too. I reread and reread his unvarnished sentences, and the more I did, the more they struck me as damnations: *You* can't focus! *You* don't follow through! *You* play not to lose! I was spinning out, I knew, but that didn't stop me from spinning out. Your sense of yourself is so provisional, so fragile, if you give it any thought for a while. Take a little time, wander down the ill-lit alleyways of your past, and you will find enough there to cobble together counternarratives to every story you have long told yourself about who you are.

I found myself thinking: Is this the real reason, however unconsciously, I had been drawn to play tennis? To discover, through playing, within the court's pressing, disclosive confines, that everything I thought about myself was untrue? That I had been hiding myself, or aspects of myself, from myself all these years? That I was, actually—take your pick, or choose them all—weak, purposeless, distracted, needy, hopeless?

36

His name was Christopher Bennett, and he had one word for me.

"Forty," he said.

"Forty," I said.

"Forty," he repeated. "I knew someone who began playing at forty who got pretty good. But not—when did you say you began playing? Mid-fifties?"

It was a Thursday afternoon in early June, and Chris, which is how he introduced himself, was walking beside me toward a court at the Cullman-Heyman Tennis Center at Yale University, where we were to play a match. It was a USTA national hard-court championship. Chris was the tournament's No. 1 seed. Chris was a four-time national champion and arguably the best hard-court player my age in the country. And as much as I was hearing Bob gently urging me to stop thinking so much about my opponent, coaxing me to abandon that old story, here Chris was beside me, built like a marine recruiter, big Wilson racquet bag on his shoulder, strolling confidently, all too real, calmly telling me it was too late. And I had to think Chris knew what he was talking about. He'd been playing tennis all his life—he'd been a successful Division I college player at Drexel in Philadelphia, and had spent his life as a teaching pro.

"I mostly like working with young players," he was telling me now, as we reached the court. He taught at the Cherry Hill Health and Racquet Club in suburban south Jersey, a half hour from Philadelphia. "Teenagers, a few of them, the serious ones—you can make a difference. After that, older than that . . . well, they *do* improve. And the ones who appreciate that, and enjoy the game, that's great."

It was shaping up as my own sort of *Groundhog Day.* I mean the Bill Murray movie, not the day. I had entered a second national Senior Slam, and, for the second time, was playing a No. 1 seed in my first match—the result, again, of winning my first match in a walkover. My initial opponent was to have been one Saeed Nowrasteh from Madison, Wisconsin, an un-seeded qualifier like me. But he withdrew with an injury. I had gotten the call from one of the tournament staff members on Wednesday night.

"That's the problem with you older guys," he'd said. "You enter a tournament, you start training for it, and you hurt yourselves."

Ha-ha-ha.

Still, it was not inevitable that I would next face the very best guy in the tourney, *again,* was it? Why was *that* becoming part of my tennis story?

It was misty, with showers in the forecast, when I set out for New Haven after breakfast the following morning. I'd received an e-mail that there would be tennis, rain or shine—that the matches would be played on the Yale Center's indoor courts if the weather was wet. This, in truth, was more bad news—though I could hear Bob telling me that it was precisely the sort of thing I had to stop thinking about. Chris Bennett had won national senior *indoor* championships. Indoor hard courts tend to play faster than any other sort of court. They are re-surfaced less frequently than outdoor hard courts and are thus worn smooth of their grit. This, plus a lack of wind and the warmth that comes with being inside, means a ball loses little speed when it bounces. Players who play well indoors hit hard.

I wasn't going to get killed. I was *really* going to get killed.

Still, there is something about being dressed to play and driving midmorning during the workweek through leafy Connecticut: It felt like playing hooky in high school. Along the Merritt Parkway, I found a college radio station, and there was Jonathan Richman, with his band, the Modern Lovers, those deadpan New England proto-punks, working his way through the song "Modern World"—rhapsodizing about, and ironizing, too, all the everyday stuff of suburban life. I rolled down the windows and sang along: "I'm in love with the modern world, now!" I glanced at my speedometer: I was doing eighty-five. Like the song, I was, I could see, something you could laugh about.

The Yale Tennis Center is situated west of the campus, in the shadow of the Yale Bowl. It was sprinkling, the sky close and yellowy gray, when I arrived at noon to register. The place looked like a contemporary Quonset hut, which is how a lot of places built to house indoor tennis courts look. I signed in and was handed a souvenir cooler bag. My match, due to start at two, would not start before three—there were only eight indoor courts, half what there were outdoors, and things were backing up. I returned to my car and drove off in search of something to eat. In one of the bleaker black neighborhoods that stretch between the Yale campus and its sports facilities, I found a Subway. There, dressed for tennis, beneath the flu-orescent lights, I ate a turkey wrap and watched the rain for a while before heading back to the tennis center.

The indoor courts at Yale are arrayed a floor below the entrance level. So when you have had your fill of examining the lobby's trophy cases, with their champion's cups and team photos—there has been tennis at Yale for a long time—you can wander around and watch from above all the smashing and dashing happening below. The place smelled of sweat, which I liked. The tournament was for players ranging in age groups from fifty to ninety, and though I saw no ninety-year-olds in action, I did feel, taking it all in, as though I was in some senior-tennis version of those paintings Titian and others did of The Ages of Man. From fifty to eighty, which was the range in ages of the players on court that afternoon, the tennis, I could see in a sweeping view, got slower, softer, and more good-natured. At some point, it became enough—more than enough—to be playing.

I pulled up a plastic chair and watched two players in the seventy-five to eighty bracket go at it. I had the sense that they'd known each other for a long time—they chatted amiably and at length during the changeovers. The play entailed a lot of slicing, and there was not much pace to the serves or flatly hit ground strokes, but the points were long, and the men moved each other around. There was a point in the ninth game of their first set (they were tied 4–4) I'll never forget. The fellow just then on the side of the net closest to where I was sitting looked every bit his age: His back was slightly hunched; his skin, dampened by perspiration, was pale and papery; and he seemed shrunken in his old and yellowed tennis whites. He received a slice serve, returned it deep with a high arc, took a short ball sent back to him, chipped it, and continued to net. His opponent, moving in, lobbed him beautifully. He turned and ran back toward the baseline, but there was no running this ball down. He stopped just below me, bent down, and clutched the bottom of his shorts—point lost—then looked up and caught my eye.

"I still have pretty good legs," he shouted up to me. "But they're not *that* fucking good." He winked and grinned like a vaudevillian. I felt one of those warm smiles crossing my face that's bigger, broader than the moment that caused it.

The rain stopped midafternoon and the sun broke through, and Chris Bennett and I were on a court outside by 4 p.m. Even with fifteen minutes of warm-ups, we were through in an hour. He hit with the kind of pace I only encounter when Kirill plays his game—I had to grip my racquet more tightly than I normally do just to keep it from being knocked off its path by his biggest shots, an adjustment that deadened my returns. He could put most shots precisely where he wanted. His serves, by my reckoning, were consistently in the nineties—at times approaching 100 mph—and often with biting spin. He would serve out wide to my backhand in the deuce court, I would slice it back feebly, and he'd move in and hit an inside-out forehand to the opposite corner: winner. He would serve into my body (backhand side) in the ad court and the point would unfold much as it had on the deuce side. I tried running around my backhand but couldn't get there. I tried chipping and charging, but his passing shots were hard, low, and accurate. He held his serves with ease.

I served well, too, by my standards—that is, consistently and in the mid-eighties often enough on my first serve. I hit a number of service winners, and elicited, exactly once, a "good serve" from Chris. There were longer points when I was serving, and the games were more all-court. I'd win a couple of points most games. Chris simply missed from time to time; I suspected he was trying out shots, practicing for his next round. I was successful coming to net one or two times. I got to deuce with him twice—as I had gotten to deuce twice in my match at Forest Hills—but he was not going to lose any points that mattered, not against me. He was a superb tennis player. He won 6–0, 6–0.

Chris went on to win the tournament, dropping only one game in the final. It was becoming clear to me that there was a kind of royalty to these national tournaments—a handful of guys who dominate, guys like Chris and Bob Litwin and Geoff, too, who'd beaten me at Forest Hills; guys who had been winning Senior Slams for thirty years. Before my match with Chris got started, I'd watched a bit of a match indoors between players my age who were qualifiers like me. They were good, the guys I watched, but they were not good enough to double-bagel me. Leaning against the tiled wall as I showered after my match, my groin muscle on my left side aching—I'd felt it tug when Chris nicely back-footed me during a brief rally—I convinced myself that I would sooner or later face a player who wasn't a top seed in one of these tournaments. It would be competitive, meaningful in some way, fun. It struck me, too, that Bob would approve of my thought process and outlook.

I stepped out into the slanty, late-afternoon sunshine in time to see Chris driving off in his Porsche. We waved and went our ways.

37

I spent my last couple of Skype sessions with Bob working on my "new" story.

"Do you know the Japanese word *shoshin,* Gerry?" he began one morning. He didn't wait for my no. "It's a word Zen teachers use. It means 'child's mind,' or 'beginner's mind.' It's that child's ability to be in the present moment, not be searching in the past, or worrying about how things will play out in the future. The child is open fully to that present moment, to being present, to finding that *wowness* in the moment. That's how I want you to be, where I want you to get to, when you are playing tennis.

"So, how are we going to get you there?" he went on to ask. Again, there was no waiting for an answer. "First, I want you to find a way not to bullshit yourself." I smiled into my computer screen at him: I liked that segue from Zen. "Your story needs some real cleaning up."

Bob believed there were things I could build on, "positives" I'd "surfaced" in my previous conversations. He liked that I was eager to learn, to improve. "But," he said, "can you be the kind of person on court who can learn from his opponents? From his losses? Because that is where a lot of learning happens, but I don't hear that from you."

He then told me about his recent loss at the tournament he'd gone off to play, to Larry Turville, like Bob a many-time senior champion and, unlike most everyone, a four-time senior world champion. The match was on clay, where Turville excels, and Bob had decided, he explained, to try a different approach than he normally had when playing him on that surface. (He'd lost to Turville a month earlier on clay, 6–3, 6–0.) "I was going to serve and volley more," Bob said. "I was going to stay away from rallying with him from the baseline, which hadn't worked. I had thought about serving and volleying for weeks, figuring I might meet him in this tournament. I had devised a new strategy. So, good story: I had learned from my opponent and was open to something new."

He paused and took a sip from his coffee mug. Then he leaned back, looked up toward his ceiling with his hands behind his head, and smiled before looking back into his screen, at me. "So what happened: I serve and volley on the very first point, and I win it. And then, I abandoned it. I think I served and volleyed one more time the entire match. And I lost 6–4, 6–2.

"What is the point of this story?" No waiting for an answer. "The point is: I had a strategy but I didn't execute it. And I didn't execute it because in the weeks before I played Larry I didn't *practice* it. I thought about what I would do but I didn't practice doing it, didn't make it a part of me, of my game. And if you don't consciously act on something, the old game—the old story—just finds a way of coming back.

"Here's something Buddha said: 'An idea that is developed and put into action is more important than an idea that exists only as an idea.' Sounds so simple, right? So obvious. But putting ideas into action is hard. Changing your way of being on court is hard.

"You want," he said, "to write a new story that you can act upon and *want* to act upon."

I asked him how he felt about losing. I told him about getting crushed up at Yale.

"Hey, losing is just part of playing. And we're playing, Gerry. We're out there. I was more upset with not having practiced that serve-and-volley. But you know what? I forgave myself for that. I never could forgive myself in tennis. For years I was someone who just berated himself. But I made it part of my mission to change that. And I mostly have.

"That's what it's about, writing your new story: Who do you want to be out there? Who do you want to be?"

38

I'd asked Bob if he could send along anything he'd written that could guide me in writing my "new story." He pointed me to a post about himself that he had up on his website. I read it after dinner one night:

I love finding the positive experience regardless of the outcome. I love searching to find the quiet within the storm. Finding relaxation in the midst of a perceived stressful situation. Developing my craft. New ways to hit the ball. New places on the court. Having a sense of purpose for each and every shot . . .

There was more, much more. I got it. I was not at all sure that this was me—actually, I was pretty sure it wasn't—but I got it.

The next day, over a sandwich at my desk at work, I opened a file on my computer and wrote four sentences that you could call goals for my tennis game, or could call three lies about myself I wish were true with one last statement that's sort of true:

I find pleasure in being patient and satisfaction in being focused.

I care about playing the point, not results of the match.

I am on court to play tennis, not to play against someone.

I am happy to play, and optimistic about improving.

I e-mailed what I'd written to Bob. I got an e-mail back from him within an hour: "Good stuff. I wrote some more. Print this story out. Read it a lot. Read it to others. Make this story the place you are going with your game."

Bob added the following to my new story:

I play to grow.

Tennis and pleasure go hand in hand for me. No matter how I play, whether I win or lose, I experience the joy of working on my game, both inner and outer.

I play in the present and this state of focus helps my performance, my freedom from anguish, and my growth as a player and a person.

I love to compete as much as or more than I love to win.

I accept my results with dignity and class. I make no excuses. I respect and appreciate my opponents, knowing that they are my teachers.

I play in joy, knowing that every time I step on the court I grow.

He also sent along an attachment: a worksheet he wanted me to print out and fill in every time I practiced or played. I was to write down my new-story list in the left column, and, in a row of boxes next to each entry, rate 1–5, with five being the highest, how I did: how patient I was, how focused, how accepting of the results . . .

I carried a printout of my new story in my tennis bag, and for a week, then another, then another, I read it before every practice I had with Kirill and every match I played. (I did not read it to others, but amused myself driving to matches and thinking of friends I might phone and begin reading it to.) And I filled out my chart, too—I filled up three of them—each time I finished hitting or playing. But I wasn't really getting anywhere. And I was wondering how playing tennis had morphed into a kind of therapy. I was feeling frustrated, burdened. I thought of calling Bob. He'd ended our final Skype session with an invitation to be in touch anytime to discuss my story. But I knew what he would say: Be patient, it takes time to shed your old story. And, anyway, I had initiated things with him. *I* had wanted to take my game to see a therapist.

39

The Amackassin Club in Yonkers is one of America's old-est tennis clubs, founded in 1888 on a ridge above the Hudson River, with a view of the Palisades across it. Its six red-clay courts and old pile of a tennis house are situated in a neighborhood where you can still glimpse the bones of what had been—huge Victorian homes, now sided with aluminum, mostly, and, in many cases, apparently divided into multifam-ily dwellings, in a Yonkers that is today, and has been for years, a small and poor American city. A good deal of the signage on the nearby shopping street I drove up was in Spanish, the cafés and restaurants promising Guatamalan or Honduran lunch specials. The club—tennis itself—seemed foreign to the place now, out of time. But tennis has a way of always seeming out of time.

I parked up the street from the club and kept the car idling. It was a summery afternoon, and I was going to sit in air-conditioned comfort and read over my Bob-infused new story a few times. I would be playing one of my last team matches of the spring, before the kids got out of school and club members began heading off here and there on their family vacations. I read my first goal over and over again, chanting it aloud to myself like a mantra: *I find pleasure in being patient and satis-faction in being focused.* I found myself thinking of how terrible I'd been as a child at praying—bored, distracted, unconvinced. This was, of course, not Bob's idea of being focused.

My opponent that afternoon, Dennis, was twenty years or so younger than me, provided some or another service to hedge funds, and, like me, had been playing tennis for only five or six years, which he mentioned as we talked a bit before starting our match. I could see right off, warming up, that he was an athlete: He was quick and coordinated. (It turned out, I'd learn from him after the match, that he'd played soccer at Bowdoin.) I could also see that his was a pusher's game of getting everything back, high-arced and deep. I tried to focus on not focusing on how I couldn't stand playing the kind of long, paceless points I was about to play. I thought about how being patient would allow me to remain just as long as I liked on this lovely red-clay court in the gilding sunshine of a June day.

I served first, was broken, and then Dennis held: Quickly I was down 0–2. Every ball Dennis hit was up-up-up and every point was going on too long for me—going on until I decided to take a big cut at one of his slow-paced, high-bouncing balls and drive it a half foot long. And then, from I know not where, it came. I couldn't name what the "it" was at first. I served crazy good in the third game: an ace and two winners. In the fourth, I won the two long rallies there were and broke Den-nis. I could sense a relaxing, physically in my shoulders and hitting arm, and psychologically in an understanding that I wasn't going to be routed. I sensed patience. During the cross-over, toweling myself after holding in the fifth game, one of Bob's Zen terms came to me: *Kaizen,* a commitment to grad-ual but constant improvement. Slowly, I was overcoming my impatience—which, in so many ways in life, had served me, trying to get from where I happened to be to where I wanted to be; but which had hampered me, too, as tennis was making clear. Slowly, I was growing patient, and liked it.

I got off the baseline in the sixth game, chipping and charging on Dennis's second serves. I broke him again, and won the next two games, too. The balls coming toward me seemed bigger, and time seemed to be slowing down. My legs felt light, my grip loose. I kept the ball up the middle, alternating my forehands, hitting flat and then with what topspin I can muster with my Eastern grip. Nothing but reading has ever come naturally to me, whatever that means, but striking a tennis ball now felt as natural as an act could be. For the first time in a tennis match, I was experiencing that state of unself-conscious hyper-focus and effortlessly melded awareness, agency, and action that the Hungarian psychologist Mihaly Csikszentmihalyi identified as *flow.*

It took two hours and fifteen minutes to complete two sets—the points were *that* long—but I won both of them, 6–2, 6–3. It mattered that I had won, but it mattered more, much more, that I had flowed for a time. This feeling I had would fail to visit me in my final team match the following week (I'd be beaten down by a twenty-something power player), and I doubted if I ever would feel quite that way—that *good*—in a singles match again. For a while I had danced with tennis, and tennis had danced with me, and it was a happy high. I texted Barbara and told her I'd won and said I'd be home soon. Then I got on line with a bunch of kids across the street from the courts and bought a Popsicle from an ice-cream truck.

40

In the beginning—years ago now, when I'd begun to hit with Kirill—I'd only played doubles. Doubles, at a club level, has a way of gently masking your weaknesses: You use your backhand less, and mostly slice with it; you can get away with simply, slowly spinning in your serve, if you keep it toward the middle of the court, "up the T," and rob your opponents of the chance to create sharp angles with their returns. You run less, too, which makes it appealing for aging men and women. Doubles games at my club (and I have found this to be true at other clubs) were also easier to find and maintain, week in and week out. The club encouraged them, helped you find a game. Doubles is *social,* which is what a tennis club is about.

I met a group of young guys—a pair of brothers, their brothers-in-law, and others—and played early Saturday- and Sunday-morning games with them every weekend my first summer at the New York Athletic Club. There was an up-before-sunrise winter game indoors with *Times* colleagues for a time; for years now I've had a Saturday-morning game indoors, October through April, with players my age from the town's country club. I love doubles, always have, and wasn't half bad. One recent summer I'd played a season-long weekly round-robin doubles—partnering with three or four different players at my club each night but accumulated points individually—and earned a second-place trophy. But I was still working with Kirill to improve my game—or thought I was—to become the best singles player I could be. I wanted to measure myself against an opponent and against the player I had been a month ago. I wanted to run, fast and toward something, while I still could.

All the serving I'd done in those spring-long team matches, though, had left my shoulder achy. And the thrashing in New Haven I'd gotten from Chris Bennett had been a reality check on just how far I could take my game. I was tired, too, I was coming to think, of being alone out there all the time, coming up short, or worse, with nowhere to hide and no one to turn to. Maybe I wanted, or even needed, someone with me on my side of the net—someone sharing the challenge, the downs, and, for that matter, the ups: a partner.

A problem with club doubles—and another reason I'd kept my focus on singles—is that you never get to develop a real partnership with a player, even at the league level, at least where I play. You play with a different partner every match. I've partnered with guys I'd never met before we introduced ourselves while popping open a can of balls. To watch a good doubles team is to see two players moving as one around the court, intuiting where a shot is going to arrive and who should take it and where the return of that shot will be directed. That takes time. There's also the matter of attitude, temperament: You want to be playing with someone you *like* on court, or at least understand—someone whose strengths and weaknesses you know (and *he* knows, as he knows yours); someone you can encourage (and be encouraged by); someone you are not going to get frustrated with (and who will not get frustrated when you blow a volley or double fault in a tight spot).

I always made time whenever attending the U.S. Open or some other tournament to watch the Bryan brothers play, the Bryans being the best doubles players in men's tennis, and the best American men's tennis has had to offer since the days of Pete Sampras. I'd seen them in March at Indian Wells beat fellow Americans John Isner and Sam Querrey in a long (for doubles) semifinal match that included a remarkable point that lasted longer than a minute by my count and took thirty-one shots to complete, the players charging, crisscrossing, scrambling for lobs, parking on the baselines, then charging again before Isner could not bend his basketball-big-man frame low enough to fetch a slice volley down the middle at his feet. And I can still see the Bryans, Bob and Mike, at point's end, locking gazes and smiling those Southern California smiles of theirs as we in the stands rose and roared.

I wanted a point like that. I wanted the camaraderie that followed, I remember telling myself at the time. And on a warm Sunday morning, in a doubles match that would change how I thought about doubles, I got all that, or *something* like that.

My partner that morning was Alton. He was an orthopedic surgeon, an arm and hand specialist, and a very good one: When I'd first met him, years before, I'd recognized him from a big special advertising insert that ran each year in the *Times Magazine,* a listing of New York "Super Docs." He, like me, worked with Kirill—his kids did, too—and we would see each other coming and going from private lessons, and hit together from time to time in one or another of the group clinics Kirill ran. He was nine or ten years younger than me, but even as he entered his fifties—and despite the gravity of the work he performed all hours of the day and night—he remained youthfully sunny, with an open face and longish, sun-bleached hair.

The headband or bandana he would wear to keep the hair out of his eyes when he was on the court, and the smile he easily flashed, and the terrific shape he was in—he played a lot of ultimate Frisbee along with the tennis—enhanced that quality of youthfulness. He was easy to be around. And he could play, had speed and stamina and solid ground strokes—had played on his high-school team back in Texas, where he grew up, the son of an oilman.

It was a day or two after getting double-bageled by Chris Bennett when I bumped into Alton at the AC and asked him if he'd be interested in entering a doubles tourney coming up at the club. The annual Century Doubles, it's called. The combined ages of each team has to add up to more than one hundred. We would make one hundred with years to spare if he was game. And he was.

41

That point: It *was* a long point, especially for a doubles point in a club match: nine shots. And it did end with my hitting a clean winner that won a crucial game. So maybe it would have stuck with me anyway, though I don't think so. I tend to forget points, games, scores of sets, all of it, unless I write it down immediately—get back to my car or into my racquet bag and get out a Moleskine notebook of the sort that's always with me. Not that I keep most of them or go back and read over the ones I have kept.

It wasn't the shot I hit. It's what came right after.

Alton and I had made it to the consolation final of the Century Doubles. (The team that eventually won the event was composed of a guy my age and a forty-year-old partner who had played for Duke.) The tournament began on a near-perfect early summer Saturday morning. There were thirty-two teams entered, men in whites of all shapes and sizes arrayed across all the club's main courts, carefully tended to for the event. Alton and I began our first-round match at eleven, and lost in a third-set tiebreak—a match, like so many in tennis, that came down to a point here or there, a ball out by a hair, a deflating net-cord winner against us at ad out in a deuce game.

I guess it was heartbreaking, in sports-ese, but didn't feel that way. We played well, played well *together*, urging, coaxing, assuring, and, on the points played best, switching and moving to spots as if we'd been partners for years.

And we would get to play on. The loss tossed us into the consolation half of the draw with fifteen other teams. We played again that afternoon, and won easily in straights, three and one. And then I biked home, jelly-limbed in the late-afternoon heat, knowing I would be playing again the following morning. It was a good feeling: being in a tournament and continuing on. Having won stayed with me longer. And I sensed I was caught up in a narrative, the ending of which was not yet known, but that I would play a part in writing—but a smaller part, it being doubles. When I woke the following morning, there was none of that barely controlled sense of panic I felt before playing singles in a tournament.

We won again that Sunday morning, and once more that afternoon, too—a grueling match that, like our first one, went to a third-set tiebreak. Our opponents were strong net-rushers: all serve-and-volley, chip-and-charge. I was pretty much gassed by the end, and Alton was carrying us, looping topspin backhands down at their feet as they charged and serving out of his mind. We won on a point we had no business winning. I smacked a service return (from the ad court) down the line: a sneaky shot; an ill-advised shot (inside-out forehands off a serve are very low percentage); an I'm-exhausted-and-want-this-thing-over shot. It would have sailed long but their guy at the net raised his racquet and nicked it. We'd be coming back the next Sunday. We'd made the consolation final.

Alton and I didn't speak that week. There was no strategizing to our game—no talk of serving out of an *I* formation (with the net player crouched in the middle and able to pounce left or right), or receiving with both of us back. Neither did we talk strategy on court, between points, as some of our opponents did. We both followed our first serves to the net, and occasionally our second serves. We poached when the opportunity presented itself, and sometimes (in my case) when it didn't. We were both pretty quick; we could scramble and cover the court: That was our game.

It worked during the first set of our final. We served to begin, then broke them, jumped to a 3–0 lead, and went on to win 6–3. They were good, our opponents. The younger of the two, CJ, a local cable-sports announcer, was one of the club's best forty-something doubles players. His partner, Andy, was a few years younger than me—a solid net player and a fierce competitor whose game included a liberal dose of yelling and taunting, either to psych himself up or get in your head or, I suspect, both, along with motivations best left to those professionally trained to understand such things. The games were close but we were making fewer errors. Sitting courtside on a bench with my own thoughts before the start of the second set, I made a mental checklist: *Never returned better up the middle—keep it up. Go for more on second serve. Stay focused.*

And just like that, my focus drifted. I'd spotted Steve among the thirty, forty club members on the veranda, watching our match. Some were waiting to play. Steve wasn't waiting to play. He was seated in street clothes, and overdressed for the weather. Steve, my neighbor; Steve, who'd loaned me a racquet when I first began to play, who had lovely strokes, as did his wife and daughters, who'd played college tennis—Steve was battling for his life. He had withdrawn from the Century Doubles exactly a year ago with stomach cramps. It turned out to be colon cancer, advanced. He had been less than a year from retiring, and he and his wife were readying their house for sale, making plans for Florida. I'd seen him from time to time over the winter bundled up and circling our cul-de-sac slowly, getting some air. We'd talked a bit in the way men are no good at. Chemo had left him wizened, wan.

I netted two returns and they held to begin the second set. Then I had my serve broken in the second game—two double faults, having served twice in the first set without one. "You're rushing, man," Alton said to me after the game. "Deep breath. Slow down."

Then, in the third game, CJ poached and drilled Alton with a volley (off another lousy return of mine—this one a fluttering backhand slice). It caromed off his shoulder, and CJ immediately apologized, in the way tennis players do. Which is to say he was happy with his excellent poach, though he had not been aiming at Alton's shoulder. But now Andy was yelling to CJ, plenty loud enough for Alton and everyone else to hear, that there was no need to apologize, that this was about *killing them*. Immediately, I could sense that Alton was unnerved (which no doubt was Andy's point, or part of it). He took a couple of big forehand swings that sailed long by plenty. "He's too excited! *Too* excited!" Andy bellowed into the otherwise peaceable morning. We were soon down 0–3.

But Alton then held (barely, in a deuce game), and we eventually gathered ourselves and broke back at 3–5, held at 4–5 to even the score, and after they then worked to hold to go up to 6–5, had the ball on our racquet to get to 6–6 and force a tiebreak. And it was in that game, with Alton serving at 40–15, that I had that point—that game changer, in the most expansive sense of that overused sports phrase.

1.) Alton served to Andy's backhand. 2.) Andy lofted a lob over my head. 3.) Alton covered (as I slid along the net to the deuce court) and struck a forehand back to Andy. 4.) Which

CJ poached and drop volleyed into the ad court. 5.) Which I slid back over and half volleyed into their deuce-court alley. 6.) Which CJ retrieved and lobbed deep into our deuce court. 7.) Which Alton hustled to get and hit a forehand into their ad court, following it to net. 8.) Which Andy, having moved to the ad court on CJ's poach, lobbed over Alton.

I ran on a diagonal from the net on the ad side and chased down the ball in the deuce-court alley. It's remarkable, at least to me, just how much information you can process—midpoint and on the run in a tense match—after you've been playing for a number of years. The lob had a high arc. I had no problem running around the ball, so I'd be able to hit a forehand. I understood we were up by two points (40–15), so going for a risky shot was not unreasonable. I glimpsed that both CJ and Andy (who had followed his shot in) were crowding the net and cheating to the center a step or two, creating a wall up the middle. I reasoned that in pressure situations, opponents often don't register, or forget that they had previously registered, that I am left-handed. I had positioned myself to rip a forehand down the line into the alley that Andy would have to spear with a backhand lunge volley—one of the toughest shots in tennis. I'd have to brush up the back of the ball a bit more and create greater topspin, for net clearance, than I usually do: The net is six inches higher at its ends than in the center. I bent my knees, took my racquet back a little farther than usual, and went for it.

It was past him before he could stick his racquet up. Clean winner. Game.

There was applause from the veranda. I stood for a second watching the ball bound off the back fence: When you're a late learner like me, and hit that rare, fine shot, you glimpse, as no one else can, all the accrued ugliness behind it—the mistimed shanks, the over-hit drives, the pathetic frame jobs I've hit. Then Alton ran to me and grabbed my shoulders with his hands, his racquet in his right one. "*That's* what I'm talkin' about!" he shouted into my face and shook me. "*That's* what I'm talkin' about!" I'd heard that expression before, and understood that he was conveying—with more than his words—his giddy approval of my shot. What I had a growing awareness of, though, was something bigger: that this was a determinatively satisfying sports moment for me that I was sharing with another soul, a man I liked and respected, and it wasn't going to go bad.

"We are not going to lose," I said quietly to Alton.

"No, we are not," he replied.

We won the tiebreak easily enough, 7–4. Another smattering of applause. Alton and I hugged; then I shook hands with CJ and with Andy, who seemed already restored to civilian friendliness. I chatted with Alton a bit in that we-won post-match say-something way. Then I grabbed my towel and racquet bag and bounded up to the veranda to find Steve. It turned out he'd left shortly after the second set began. (He would die the following spring.)

I texted Barbara, who was swimming her Olympian laps in the club's big pool and would check her phone whenever. I then wandered out through the back of the tennis house and past the snack bar and down a grassy slope to an arrangement of Adirondack chairs positioned for a view of Long Island Sound. I slumped into one of them and gazed out on the water, lapping lazily, sequined by the late-morning sun. I could sense my exhaustion and my relief, and smell a mix of June-warmed lawn and salt tang off the sound and my own drying sweat. I breathed it in deeply, everything. I was by myself, familiarly enough, but didn't feel alone, not alone at all.

42

John was the best player in town my age, one of the best sixty-something players for miles around. I'd gotten to know him long before I'd had any idea I'd be playing tennis. We'd served for years on the local library board together. He was an education-industry executive, working at Scholastic and then at a start-up that provided services that might improve the quality of school principals and other administrators. We'd have a drink from time to time after a board meeting; we knew people in common (my friend Paul, for one), shared interests, liked each other. We must have talked a little about tennis: I knew he'd gone to Colorado College and played tennis there, and had grown up in the Chicago suburbs in a family that played tennis. I remember him telling me about a lakeside summer home, where, as a boy, he watched his grandfather play on Sunday mornings. All the men were in white flannels.

John played at the country club, and over the years, after I'd begun playing, we'd found ourselves in doubles matches together there. He was awfully good, a 5.0 player in his younger days. (We played singles once; he crushed me 6–0, 6–2.) He was a small, trim man, nearly bald, with the serve—a hard, flat, knifing serve—of someone taller. He followed it to net, slicing his approach shots low and carving his volleys like someone who had learned early and well and played at a high level. He told me one afternoon about how he'd hit everything with a Continental grip back in college in the early '70s—that's how the game was still being widely played back then, serve-and-volley and no grip change. It wasn't until he was in his early fifties that he'd got an instructor and rebuilt his forehand, brought his grip around to Eastern to generate some topspin. It took years, he told me—frustrating, discouraging years. Here was an aspect of his game I could relate to.

John organized a doubles match at the country club one Sunday afternoon in late July, a few weeks after the Century Doubles tourney, and I biked over straight from my session with Kirill at my club, the NYAC. I was playing crazy amounts of tennis: the private lessons, a group clinic, singles matches on Tuesday nights, doubles matches on Thursday nights, and whatever else I could squeeze in on weekends. When you are playing better, there's the urge to play more. And doubles took a lot less out of me. We played three sets that afternoon at the country club, rotating partners. It was fun, and more than fun when I partnered with John: He raised my game, as a better player will do. There was no mental energy sapped by being frustrated with a weaker partner's muffed volleys or poor shot selection. There was no responsibility to be the stronger half and carry the team. And there was the confidence that comes with a better player's belief in you. You make shots because you *think* you will make them because *he* thinks you will make them.

"First serve in, right now, partner," he would command, in his quietly warm way, looking over his shoulder toward me at the baseline as he took up his position at the net. And in it would go. A significant part of the tennis court extends between your ears.

An idea had come to me as John and I played together that afternoon, and after, as we gathered our things and walked toward the parking lot, I tried it on him: Would he like to enter the national grass-court championships at Forest Hills in September with me? Go as a doubles team? He'd think about it, he said. But not too long: He e-mailed me the following morning to say he was in.

43

John and his wife, Pamela, would be spending time in August at their place in Vermont; and Barbara and I were heading to Maine for ten days: There wasn't going to be any time, really, to train together for the grass nationals. We spent one long, sweltering Saturday afternoon together with Kirill, who ran us ragged chasing his lobs and blasted forehands at us as we created a wall at the net, or tried to. And we entered a member-guest tournament at my club, in which we were to play a single set against two different teams, advancing to a next round if we won both. We won our first 6–4, then ran into a pair of youngish guys maybe just a dozen years removed from being doubles partners at Fairfield University in Connecticut. They had blistering first serves and tricky, kicking second serves; and they had Division 1 volleys, and the reach and reaction time to punch offensively at balls you were sure you put in nonreturnable places. But their going for too much on big points and our hanging on and hanging in made a not unrespectable set of it, with a number of deuce games. We lost in the end, 6–2. Somehow—and I will go to my grave remembering this—I held my serve twice.

During the August weeks I was in town, Kirill and I worked

on those shots most important to have for doubles. I practiced volleying, with a focus on my weakest, the backhand up near my shoulder: if I remembered to get my right, non-hitting hand up behind the racquet, fingertips pressed against the strings, I'd keep from swinging and thus properly punch the ball. I practiced the offensive forehand lob with topspin, designed to keep going once it bounced, the harder to chase down; and the defensive backhand lob with underspin, designed to slow things down and keep you in a point.

I practiced overhead smashes, staring up into the glinting skies of high-summer afternoons, turned sideways in a kind of trophy pose to angle them into the alleys, positioning myself, as Kirill instructed, so that it seemed the ball would drop down directly at the back of my head. I practiced not getting too frustrated when I drove one smash after another too wide or into the net. Thwarted, crestfallen, even betrayed: Missing an overhead can fill you with sour feelings. Maybe it's that what should be an obvious winner becomes so quickly a lost point. Maybe it's that it is all too apparent that it is all on you—the waiting on everyone's part and then your sudden, accelerated aggression—and you just swung and missed and utterly failed. "Never hit three overheads in a row," Kirill advised during one of our Saturday sessions. "If somehow they return two of your smashes, let the third one bounce and hit a forehand or, if you are at the net, a little drop volley. No one hits three overheads in a row without missing. Missing that third one will kill you."

In my sessions with Kirill, hitting and listening, I was becoming increasingly aware of how doubles is more a game of angles and ball placement. I worked on this aspect of my game on Sunday mornings, in a group session Kirill organized. There would be four of us, the cast rotating depending on vacations or weekends away, and Kirill would set us up on court two to a side and run us through drill after drill. We practiced how to lob and how to switch when we'd been lobbed. We practiced poaching, which I loved when I was at the net, cutting off a ball intended for my partner—especially if I could dart from the deuce court to the ad court and take the volley on my forehand, angling down at the opposing net player's feet or wider, into the alley. And then there was what came to be my favorite drill: Both opponents at the net, my partner at the net, too, and me back but inside the baseline two or three feet, as I might be if I were working my way to net. Kirill would feed balls to the opponents, who were to volley deep toward me. I was to get low, lean forward with my arms outstretched, and be prepared to strike those volleys "on the rise," just as they began coming up from their bounce, and drive them low, up the middle. This meant shortening my backswing, bringing the racquet forward in a sort of scooping motion, and, most of all, remaining intensely focused. There was *no time.*

In the hour we scheduled on Sunday afternoons, Kirill and I would work on my serve-and-volley. Singles tennis is very much a side-to-side game; doubles, I was learning, is mostly forward and back. Coming in behind your serve starts with getting the service toss right—out in front of you, so you are chasing the ball inside the baseline. I was to hit a spin serve into the returner's body or up the T; a hard, flat serve would not give me time to move in and get set; a serve out wide would give the returner the chance to angle a return to my alley that I'd never reach. Placing my spin serve came easily enough to me. So did hopping off my landing leg and beginning my rush forward. What I could not remember to do was stop. Once I'd served I was to bolt two or three steps to the service line and then, at the moment the returner was about to make contact with the ball, do a split-step and prepare myself for a volley. But time and again I just kept running. The thing is, I actually thought I *was* stopping, or, anyway, slowing. We had the following exchange many times and for weeks running:

"You ran through the volley, Gerry."

"I didn't."

"You did. You just stopped when you volleyed. Which you were not set to do. You have to stop *before* you volley—split-step—and then step toward the ball, right or left, and punch it."

It's clear—from neuroscience and experience—that the aging brain takes longer to collect and compute data to the body, and that the aging body takes longer to absorb this data on the muscular level, especially under pressure. This is why older drivers shouldn't go too fast, and why older students of tennis don't know half the time where their legs and excitement are carrying them.

44

On the last Friday afternoon of August—hot, cloudless, breezeless—John and Pamela and Barbara and I met up at the U.S. Open. The Tennis Center grounds were overcrowded with fans getting an early start on Labor Day weekend, many of them sipping vodka-laced drinks from large plastic cups as the sun and heat and sweetened vodka turned them roseate, loud-voiced, and puzzleheaded. We wended our way to Court 6, one of a set of three, small, newly reconstructed outer courts, adjoined for the viewer by steep banks of bleachers behind the baselines that allowed for glimpsing action on the courts to the left or right. The bleachers were only half-filled, though the match was scheduled to begin in ten minutes. Not many people cared about this one—unless you were, say, a couple of guys in their sixties transfixed by the ability of a player just days from his forty-second birthday to win still and often at the top of the pro doubles game.

Daniel Nestor had played more than 1,300 doubles matches on the men's tour. He had eighty-five career titles with eight different partners; he had won doubles titles at each of the four Grand Slams at least once, and had taken home a gold medal at the 2000 Olympics in Sydney, playing for Canada,

where his parents had immigrated (from the former Yugoslavia) when he was a small boy. Nestor had reached No. 58 as a singles player in the '90s, but had found his best game later, as a doubles partner. Only Bob and Mike Bryan had more career wins, and now, in middle age as 2014 drew to a close, he was ranked No. 4.

Nestor was a marvel of economy and precision, as his partner this day and on many others, Nenad Zimonjic—another great doubles specialist, from Serbia, and no youngster either, at thirty-eight—would be quick to tell you, and as we, and their unseeded Colombian opponents, were about to see. Nestor was left-handed, and his serve was reminiscent of lefty John McEnroe's: his right foot parallel to the baseline, his bow to begin his service motion deep, his toss high, his back arched and turned to the net, his swing relaxed, his goals to concoct just the right admixture of slice (severe) and pace (not too much) to a) buy himself the time to get to net unhurried and b) through careful placement (into the body, up the T), rob his serve's returner of a good clean whack at the ball. And then there were his volleys when he was positioned at the net. There, he would occupy himself in the moments before a point commenced by doing a kind of tai chi, half-swinging his racquet gently over and over and swaying in slow motion. Then he'd step close to the net, extend his arms forward in the ready position, and achieve instantly an alert stillness that had about it something of the auratic. Little got past him. His volleys were seldom fierce. He preferred tenderly directing the ball just beyond his opponents' reach. Touch, placement, killing softly: The Colombians were dispensed quickly and quietly, 6–2, 6–2.

"A day at the office," John said, as we all descended the bleachers, and Nestor chatted amiably courtside with the sort of appreciative fans (oldsters, mostly) who make such good

company watching outer-court tennis matches in the early stages of a tournament. I knew what he meant. I was thinking about Nestor's approach, too, his mind-set, or what I imagined it to be: that heightened but calm focus he brought to *this* point, *that* volley; that solitude he seemed to achieve, even in a doubles match—he and Zimonjic barely spoke; that sense of relaxed intensity he gave off and that interest in the game and its possibilities, despite all the years on court, he continued to demonstrate with both time-honed shots and freshly improvised ones, like the time he got his racquet head on a topspin-laden ball sinking toward his midsection and somehow redirected it across the net with so much sidespin that it bounded untouched—a clean winner—toward the umpire's chair.

I wanted that, or something like it. The presence, attentiveness, and mastery. The communion with skilled practices. And that such things were, of course, out of reach—like one of Nestor's perfectly placed volleys—didn't dampen my desire for them. It can be enough, at afternoon's end, to have something to reach for.

45

He got to the right place—he's exactly where he wants to be!" she shouted. *He* was me. She was Paula Scheb, an all-American doubles player at the University of Florida a generation ago who went on to work on tennis teaching methods and strategy with Nick Bollettieri before he was the *legendary* Nick Bollettieri. For nearly twenty years now she had been director of tennis at the grand (i.e., five championship golf courses) Bonita Bay Club in Naples, Florida, and her gifts for tennis instruction had earned her the title of Master Professional from the United States Professional Tennis Association. Which is what gave her the authority to be on court in a small tennis stadium in Tucson early one cloudless and warm Saturday morning at summer's end, a lapel mike affixed to her tennis tank top, demonstrating for three dozen or so serious tennis amateurs like myself a new doubles strategy she had devised with Sujay Lama, himself a onetime all-American who now coached the women's tennis team at the University of North Texas. He was with her on court and had a lapel mike, too. But he was mostly spinning serves in quietly when Scheb told him to and listening with the rest of us while she—wiry, kinetic, forceful, but not without humor—animatedly imparted their

novel approach to doubles' court positioning and point creation, using some of us to demonstrate, or to try to.

I would be the first of us to correctly position himself as
what Scheb called the "crosscourt worker bee." I had, per her
instructions, sliced Lama's serve back to him with a backhand
from the deuce court and followed it in to net—but not *all* the
way in. Scheb and Lama believed that having both members of
a doubles team too close to the net left you mortally vulnerable to the lob. So while the non-serve-receiving "terminator"
situated herself or himself right up to the net, within four feet
or so, the worker bee was to hover back just behind the service line, there to stay and move only laterally (depending on
where an opposing player was striking the ball from) or back
in pursuit of a lob. That's where I was, a couple of feet behind
the service line and toward the alley, when Scheb grabbed my
left bicep and began praising my positioning. I had known my
place in her and Lama's new "staggered" approach.

Of course, as I would later discuss with Scheb, I could never
imagine getting back many balls from where she said I should
be—no-man's-land, between the baseline and service line,
where tennis tradition holds you seldom want to be. There,
you get caught having to absorb incoming balls down at your
shoe tops, flailing to make half volleys or low volleys, among
the more difficult shots in tennis. And should you somehow
make that half volley or volley, you are more likely than not
going to be hitting that ball softly and up, providing your
doubles opponent at the net with an easy floater to smack
back down at you. No, I'd rather get to net and run the risk
of failing to run down the occasional well-struck, topspin lob.

But standing there on court that morning, I was mostly
watching the surrounding mountains blanch away their dawn
pinkness and feeling the desert sun starting to toast my shoul-

ders and getting glowy from the attention I was getting from
Coach Scheb. *I'd done it correctly.* And then the thought struck
me: Here I was, months from my sixty-second birthday, once
again in just the sort of moment, the *only* sort of moment,
when I'd ever earned any praise when playing, or attempting
to play, a sport. In baseball practice on my Babe Ruth team,
as a thirteen-year-old playing right field, I had known exactly
where to throw a ball I'd caught—to what base or which cutoff
man. In basketball practice on my junior-varsity high-school
basketball team, working on the pick and roll, I had known
exactly how to slide off the screen I had set, move to the basket,
and take the pass from my dribbling teammate. But I'd never
gunned down a runner from right field—I couldn't throw hard
enough—and I'd never taken a pass off a screen and nailed
the open, twelve-foot jumper—I was too short to get off a
good shot that close to the hoop. I was the kid who mastered
the part of a sport that's in your head. I *understood.* (Others
executed.) I was the good student, the perpetual student, of
whatever was getting taught.

On court, in Tucson, I was, however, a happy student,
among fellow students as upbeat and eager as I was. There
were nearly 250 of us—men and women no younger than
middle-aged and, for the most part, closing in on elderly—
attending what was called, perhaps a little loftily, the U.S.
Tennis Congress. The three-day-long congress (this was only
its second annual gathering) was the brainchild of a good-
and-getting-better recreational player in his mid-forties named
P. J. Simmons. His day job was in corporate sustainability, and
though he was athletic (he'd become a certified fitness instructor in his twenties), he, like me, had come to tennis late—in
his case, at forty-one. Simmons had a blog called *The Road to
4.5 Tennis,* on which he detailed his own quest to become a

near top (USTA-rated 4.5) recreational player (a level I'd never reach, at least as a singles player) and also offered guest posts by coaches and instructors on everything from technique and strategy to fitness and nutrition. The congress was very much a real-world manifestation of the blog: three packed days, which an amateur player of a certain age would spend in the company of top teaching pros, flexibility gurus, equipment experts, and the occasional former tour player, never being taken anything less than seriously.

The setting for the congress was the Hilton El Conquistador Golf and Tennis Resort, on the outskirts of the city, though Tucson is one of those places where it's not at all clear—amid the freeways and four-lane strips with their gun shops and pawn shops and self-storage depositories and then sudden entrances to vast, treeless housing developments—just what separates center from periphery. At the El Conquistador, my room was a neo-Mission "villa" down a steep, winding path-way, up which I would trudge to reach the convention center, with its wide hallways, lined with hawkers of tennis stuff, and its refrigerated meeting rooms, where you could learn the intricacies of racquet stringing or exactly what not to ingest right before a match. There were also any number of hotel-lobby and poolside bars, along with an array of vista-suffused out-door lounge areas, where time and again I eased myself into conversations with people who, like me, were working hard to be better tennis players while in the process of rethinking or rearranging or reorienting their lives—or sensing they would soon have to—as they confronted getting older.

There was a widow who said that taking up tennis had given her days purpose and structure after her husband died, and a doctor trying to figure out how to spend fewer hours in his practice and more on the tennis court. On the congress's first full day, a Friday, I'd bumped into Amy Eddings, a long-time morning voice on my National Public Radio station. She also posted pictures and texts from time to time on a sardonic Tumblr blog she'd created, a chronicle of tennis frustrations and weirdness she called (for all of us!) *I Hate Tennis.* I asked her how her game was going, and she replied that she was leaving NPR in a few months, leaving New York, too, which for Amy meant Brooklyn. This was not the non sequitur it may seem: Tennis for players like those at the congress—players like me—was tied up with later-life stirrings and transitions, with questions of what you might be doing next and where you might be doing it. First-world problems, I can hear my younger son, Luca, saying (*like your worrying which elite law school will accept you,* I can imagine myself thinking), and it's true that such dilemmas and possibilities occupy the aging cohort of the upper-middle class who more or less resemble the couples in those ads the financial-services industry aims at them. *Invest for What's Next. Keep Good Going. So You Can Enjoy the Journey Ahead.* But healthy, financially secure sixty-one-year-olds with a perspective on just how lucky they are lie awake at night, too.

I told Amy that I can't be in a car with my wife for five minutes without the conversation drifting to my retirement or semiretirement—"downshifting"—and when we should sell our too-big-for-us suburban home and what it might be like to move to an apartment in northern Manhattan, maybe; or, perhaps, to find a small midcentury modern house in the development, Usonia, that Frank Lloyd Wright conceived and oversaw the building of thirty-five minutes north of us; or to build an eco-house farther north of us in the Hudson Valley, or even out west, in northern California—Marin or Sonoma—if life took us there. Barbara had been born in San Francisco, and our older son, Guy, was living there now, working, as it happened, as an NPR news producer. "I'm burnt out on news radio," Amy said when I mentioned this, and so, she added, was her husband, Mark, who worked as a radio-news anchor. They'd bought an old Victorian home in a small town in Ohio where her sister lived and not too far from her aging parents, and they were going to fix it up. There was a tennis court close by.

46

I'd arrived at the El Conquistador late on a Thursday after-noon after a day of air travel, and, having showered and settled in, headed to the one of the hotel's restaurants to eat dinner at the bar in the company of a book I was nearly done reading—congress activities would begin the next morning. On the way to the restaurant I'd run into my performance coach, my tennis-life guru, Bob Litwin. It turned out he was going to be giving a seminar on his thing: rewriting your tennis story. He was due for dinner in half an hour with a group of fellow coaches and instructors but had time for a drink. We slid onto stools at the lobby bar and ordered glasses of white wine.

Bob was supposed to be in Istanbul, playing for the sixty-five-and-over U.S. team in the international senior-team championships. But he'd torn a muscle in his calf. "I'm glad I'm here, or that's the story I'm telling myself," he said, and raised his glass for a clink. He'd come in from Boulder, Colo-rado, where he'd been visiting a daughter and grandchildren. He was soon telling me that he was arranging to move there. "So I'm rewriting my story big-time," he said. There were de-tails to work out with his clients back east, and thoughts of taking what he had done with New York hedge-fund guys to San Francisco (about a two-hour flight from Boulder), where there were venture capitalists and tech entrepreneurs in need of self-understanding and motivation.

"But how about you, Gerry?" he asked soon enough, re-establishing the essential dynamic of our relationship. "Your focus. Your game."

"I've had a satori," I said, throwing out a Zen term because Bob liked them, and also because I thought it carried just enough pretentiousness and out-of-placeness, given the hotel-bar tableau, to establish the half irony (or more) I am usually after when I talk about things that actually matter to me. But there was just then a raucous group whoop from a lobby banquette behind us—young people in from Texas for a wedding, it turned out, glued to a TV, celebrating a Texans score against the Colts on Thursday Night Football. Bob never heard me.

I said, starting again: "Since we last talked"—that was back in the spring—"I've been playing a lot of doubles. In tournaments and stuff. I've come to think, when it comes to tournament competition, I'm really a doubles player." I paused. He said nothing. "It's partly a physical thing," I went on to say. "Doubles is easier on my body, my joints. It's also what I guess I can get best at. I'm here to mostly work on my doubles game." I took a sip of wine. Bob leaned in. He's good at what he does. "There's more to it, actually," I went on. "Maybe I'm not yet understanding it all. There are ways, when I'm playing competitively, that playing doubles makes me less anxious, less burdened or exposed or something. Happier."

"You need to keep playing tournaments, Gerry—small ones, lousy ones," Bob said. He was going to keep it to my tennis game here at the bar. "You'll bump into jerks who won't be as open to your story—this journey you began and you're on—as the guys you have met at the nationals. Winning is desperately important to some of these guys. And you will beat them eventually because, as you get older, you will make fewer errors, and the guys you are playing won't be able to move like you."

Bob's wife snuck up behind him just then and gave him a hug, and a relaxed smile spread across his face. They were off to dinner with the congress faculty in one of the hotel's banquet rooms, and I settled up and headed along one lengthy corridor, then another, to a small, subdued Tex-Mex restaurant at the far reaches of the hotel that, at just past seven, had only a handful of diners (and would have only a few more). I took a bar stool and ordered some fish tacos and another glass of wine. On the big flat-screen above me, it was halftime in the Colts-Texans game.

The book I'd been reading all day on my dogleg flight from New York to Salt Lake to Tucson, and had just a couple of short chapters to finish, was *Happiness by Design: Change What You Do, Not How You Think,* by a British economist turned behavioral scientist named Paul Dolan. The book had a foreword by Daniel Kahneman, the Nobel Prize–winning psychologist (the award was in economics, actually, for his behavioral work) who in the late 1990s had more or less jump-started what had grown to be the most fascinating and popular (and criticized, when not dismissed) realm of social science in our time: happiness studies. It was Kahneman, in his "hedonic psychology" writings, who put forth that we should and can pay close attention to "the experiencing self"—that there were ways to research and survey how people actually felt about their own lives deep down, about what social science now calls "subjective well-being." I had been immersing myself in

happiness studies—books by Daniel Gilbert, Martin Selig-
man; Kahneman's magisterial *Thinking, Fast and Slow*. I was
reading Dolan's new book with a mind to helping me think
about why doubles-tennis competition was making me happy
and—in the way that reading at thirty-two thousand feet had
been tending to work on me—had bumped into any number
of passages that set me gazing out at the deep, airless blue and
pondering my aging life.

When cognitive and positive psychologists, neuroscientists,
contemporary philosophers, and behavioral economists like
Dolan ponder well-being, they commonly distinguish between
two types. There is what they refer to as *evaluative* well-being:
This has to do with the overall satisfaction you have with your
life, with goals achieved, successes scored. (For some researchers, there's a sort of subset of evaluative well-being, *eudaemonic*
well-being, involving an individual's perceptions of whether it
all seems to have had a meaning—whether you have lived a
valuable life.) The attainment of this kind of fulfillment is tied
up for most of us with work, a loving partner (or a succession
of them, as the case may be), kids raised well (if parenting was
desired), and financial security, along with religious faith for
those who carry it and with contributions to our communities
and the greater good. And, let's face it, it's tied up, too, with
living to a certain age: You really can't judge your life fulfilled
until you have a pretty firm sense of its shape—until enough
time has passed to construct the One Big Narrative of You (at
the risk of sounding self-helpy, which Dolan does here and
there). That's just about the time, of course, when you sense
age advancing—advancing like those shadows you watch from
your plane window, spreading across plains and hillsides in late
afternoon, as the sun lowers toward mountains to the west and
things soon enough darken to black.

The second type of happiness that social scientists seek to measure—with surveys asking people to evaluate daily experiences on a scale of 1 to 10; this is largely what leads skeptics to doubt the whole enterprise—is called *experienced* well-being. How's your commute? Your work environment? Your exercise regimen and the dinner you cook most nights? Do you enjoy playing with your kids? Talking with your spouse? Watching this season's offering from HBO? How's that *day* of yours?

Even if you believe, as I do, that it seems worthwhile to ask people how they feel about their in-the-moment well-being, you understand that measuring happiness is not like measuring the level of good cholesterol in your blood (which, in your sixties, you monitor the way you monitor how your retirement portfolio is doing against the benchmark indexes). *Experienced* well-being in the unfolding of any given day might involve qualitatively different feelings: delight, discovery, exhilaration, excitement, bliss, joy, serenity. Dolan himself makes a distinction between aroused and non-aroused states of experienced well-being: passionate afternoon sex, say, on the one hand, and the calm you feel each night because you have a job that will pay for your kids' college education. It can be difficult for an individual to sort all this out. What Dolan wants us to do (and this is a contribution to happiness literature his book provides) is precisely to get better at sorting all this out—to become more *attentive* to what we are feeling and to what makes us happy.

Dolan makes another helpful distinction: between pleasure and purpose. Both can make us happy in our daily doings—and, by the way, Dolan thinks that happiness, properly understood, is all that matters in the construction of a good life. But pleasure and purpose are different. Taking your kids to spring training—that was the last and only other time I'd been to

Tucson—is a blast. Arriving back home and getting them up and off to school on a dark, late-winter morning—homework checked, breakfast offered, lunches made, obstinate walk in the cold with them endured—is satisfying, purposeful. But no fun.

You need a balance of purpose and pleasure, Dolan maintains. He calls someone who more or less gets it right a *sentimental hedonist,* "sentimental" for him meaning not teary or mushy but being capable of purposeful actions and recognizing the emotions they engender. And munching my fish tacos, sipping my sauvignon blanc, watching Andrew Luck march the Colts down the field for a decisive score, and contemplating what the purposeful hours of tennis instruction each of the following three days would do for my game, I was feeling pretty much there. The researchers tell us that sixty-somethings are poised for happiness. The Stanford psychologist Laura Carstensen and her colleagues have posited that life satisfaction increases in late-middle age—all that career and parenting stress behind you—and that your "peak of emotional life" awaits you as you approach seventy. German neuroscientists have concluded that people in their sixties have a "reduced regret responsiveness"—we're less prone to be made unhappy by things we cannot change—and that this may be hardwired.

But it was only when, football finished, I read Dolan's brief conclusion with the last of my wine, that I got beyond happiness theory and grasped a bit of self-comprehension that had been eluding me: A way of understanding the *joy* (and not only the *satisfaction*) I'd gotten occasionally when playing singles tennis but was now regularly feeling playing doubles. Here is the sentence: "The evaluative self"—the life-arc self, that is; the fulfilled-or-not self—"is largely constructed," Dolan writes, "and I agree with Daniel Kahneman that we give it too much of a voice in determining our behavior—more than we give to our experiencing self." Okay, this might not on first read, or second or third, immediately strike one as epiphanic. It did me, though. All the hours and years I'd been striving to become a serious senior singles player, fulfilling as it had been, had been just a little too much about achievement—lonely, questing validation—and not enough about pleasure in the moment. I was, on some level, working to add a coda to the One Big Narrative of Me. Doubles was offering me something else: less pressure, less bodily strain, more companionship, more fun. Not that I didn't want to be kick-ass good at it.

I closed the book, finished my wine, and strolled back to my room under a thick blanket of desert-sky stars. I went to bed knowing myself better. Maybe. Another thing the research holds: You get to sixty or so and you're more comfortable with ambiguity, contingency, deep-going doubt.

Who knows.

47

After breakfast the following morning I found myself in a small circle of women near the El Conquistador's pool, where one of them, Bonnie, was making the case for Aleve. "Advil bothers my stomach," she said. Aleve v. Advil is for senior players what Federer v. Nadal is for tennis fans in general: the default conversation starter, the one that never gets old, if you are getting old. (Me, I prefer Advil.) It's a signal that it is time to discuss our aging muscles, tendons, and joints, which we are always eager to discuss. Detailed recaps of pulls and sprains sustained, treatment-journey narratives, lamentations of the destruction of tissue and bone: All are welcome.

I'd been sitting nearby with Bonnie's husband, George, easing my way into the first day of the tennis congress with just such a conversation. George and Bonnie had attended the first congress in Atlanta the previous year, but he would not be playing this time: He had a bad left knee and feared it might need to be replaced. He'd already had his right hip replaced. His football years at Cornell in the '60s, he told me, were catching up to him as he entered his seventies.

I'd been telling George about my left shoulder. There was tendonitis and bursitis—had been for years—but the inflammation had gotten worse, or anyway more painful. I'd gone to a sports-medicine specialist and he'd sent me for X-rays: There was no bone damage. He'd had me extend my arm out to my side, then asked me to resist as he pulled down on it with both his hands. "That's not a tear—you have plenty of strength," he told me. He suspected that there was now bicep tendonitis, too, which has a way of extending the aching down to the elbow and forearm. I didn't need an MRI. He suggested I play less, which I wasn't hearing of. He suggested I ice the shoulder after every match I played, which did provide temporary relief. He had me do strengthening exercises with a thick elastic band; those, after a few months, alleviated the pain but only a little. I went back to him and said I wanted a cortisone shot. That was keeping me on the court and wince-free most every time I served, and the fact that you served less in doubles than in singles was helping, too.

Our aging muscles and tendons ache and pull and sometimes (please, no) tear because they have been, by the time you reach your sixties, so repetitively engaged and have (as cells grow old) also become increasingly inelastic. Getting out of bed each morning is a daily reminder of this deep biology: those crinkly clicking sounds you hear back somewhere in your inner ear as your neck twists toward the clock (crepitus, brought on, most likely, by the wearing away of cartilage); the resistant stiffness in your upper back as you bend for your slippers; the overall *ungivingness* of your extremities as you straighten and extend yourself to the day. Which is why many of us attending the congress had begun the morning with a workshop devoted to stretching.

Phil Wharton describes himself as a musculoskeletal therapist. Together with his father, Jim—who calls himself an exercise physiologist, and is known in the sports world as "The

Mechanic"—he'd endeavored to increase the flexibility of countless Olympic athletes and members of big-time sports teams. His small, very fit body was evident in his snug black warm-up outfit as I entered the ballroom where he was holding his pre-breakfast stretching clinic. He had a portable training table set up in the middle of the room, and we—three dozen or so still-creaking, coffeeless souls—were handed mats and lengths of bright-blue rope by an assistant and instructed to spread ourselves in a semicircle around Phil.

As any regular practitioner of yoga (which I am not, but Barbara and every woman I seem to know is) will happily tell you, stretching is a means to knowledge, bodily knowledge. You come to understand how it all connects. Phil Wharton has his own take on this: He thinks that most athletes stretch wrong. Those runners you see in the morning with a foot up on a fence post or car trunk, knee straight and locked, grabbing their calf or toes, trying to warm their hamstrings? Their muscles, he told us, are actually contracting to protect themselves from the well-intentioned violence of the stretch. To properly stretch a muscle, you have to first *isolate* it— become conscious of it; then contract the muscle opposite it (your quadricep, say, if you are stretching your hamstring); then relax that isolated muscle (which will occur naturally when you contract the opposite muscle) before gently and quickly stretching it for no longer than two seconds. Repeat the stretch ten times and the muscle will be warmed, loosened, invigorated—ready for exercise.

We extended our wrists and flexed our fingers. We elevated our shoulders sideways and forward, rotated them internally and externally. On our backs, wrapping our ropes around one foot, then the other, we tugged gently to stretch our hip adductors (while tightening the abductors), and then vice versa. Glutes, psoai, the deep posterior spinal group, the piriformis beneath the big muscles in our buttocks and low-back rotators—all these and more got their two seconds of stretching, ten times. Then we rubbed our toes and spread our toe webbing. It was playing with yourself for every part of your body except the part that constitutes playing with yourself.

By the time the workshop was done I felt as though I didn't *need* coffee. (Well, almost.) I was ready for a full day of on-court drills. Of course, to get yourself fully stretched the Wharton way before getting on a tennis court would take a minimum of twenty minutes and could take forty-five with the toes and all. And who had *that* kind of time? Real athletes. (There were top professional players who elaborately stretched *before* heading to bed.) And, I found myself thinking, elderly athletes, retired or sort-of retired: They had all the time in the world, until time ran out. I'd read not long ago about a senior tennis champion named John Powless. Powless was in his eighties, a onetime tennis coach and basketball coach at the University of Wisconsin, long retired, and he'd won more than seventy senior tournaments. Someone was making a documentary about him. He woke up every morning at 5 a.m. and stretched for an hour.

I could imagine that. It really was a means to a kind of self-knowledge, which, after all, was what Montaigne said we should be seeking when we were done with our doing. Contemplative, ritualistic, it could, done properly, be almost a form of prayer. And a need for some kind of praying—as the months and years and aches and pains accumulated—was surely coming.

48

Howard Moore was to be my "mentor" at the tennis congress. We introduced ourselves that Friday evening at the congress's opening banquet, where I was seated next to him. He was a large fellow with a big, ruddy-and-tan face and thinning, silvery hair combed back, and was dressed like a southern gentleman: blue blazer, pale-lemon slacks, loafers, and a rep tie. We listened to P. J. Simmons formally welcome us to the congress and talk a bit about his notion that all senior players who are serious about their games benefit from being exposed to a variety of coaches and instructors. Over dinner, amid countless interruptions from coaching pals, Howard explained what being my mentor meant: During the next two days, along with all my group classes and workshops, he would be providing a couple of hours of individual instruction. In addition, he'd look in on me during my other sessions and, in general, be around for consultation. Lucky me, as it turned out: Howard would prove the most delightfully enthusiastic man I'd ever spent time with on a tennis court.

He was something of a tennis-coaching legend. He ran the tennis program at the Saddlebrook Resort in Tampa, a program that had its roots in one founded years ago by Harry

Hopman, the great Australian coach whose prize students included Rod Laver, Roy Emerson, and Ken Rosewall, among others. Hopman had trained Howard, too, when Howard was a promising junior player in England. Now Howard would be coaching me for a couple of days.

As the dinner was about to break up that Friday evening, Howard asked me if there was anything in particular I had in mind to do during our lengthy individual session the following afternoon. "I am here for you," he said. "Is there a stroke, say, we might really get to work on?"

I was trying to improve my one-handed backhand drive, I told him. I explained how I had been working on it with my teaching pro, Kirill; I explained, even as I knew Howard needed no such explanation, that while I was playing more competitive doubles than singles now, and the backhand drive was less crucial in doubles, a loopy, diving topspin drive could be a great weapon in doubles, tough to volley as it dipped over the net. Howard nodded and said, with his jolly Englishman's accent, "Yes, *absolutely*, but you have to get it to really dip with topspin." Otherwise, he was saying without saying, it crosses the net high and is vulnerable to be poached and swatted down. I was conscious then of how much I loved the intricate shoptalk of tennis, even if the intricacies under discussion were to remain beyond my ability to attain.

We kept talking about the one-hander, the brutal mechanics that went into the loveliest of shots. It alone among hard-hit ground strokes is struck with a grip that places the palm in front of the racquet, not behind it, where it can absorb the impact of the ball and stabilize things. Your hitting arm is in front of your body in a closed (sideways-facing) stance, not behind it, as it is with a forehand. As a result, the stroke doesn't engage the big, strong muscles (those of the chest; the bicep) like a forehand but mainly the muscles behind the shoulder, where my tendonitis and bursitis can smart with a swing. It's also a shot where the racquet must meet the ball well out in front of you, and away from your body to the side, in order to get under it, come up the back of it, and achieve topspin. Taking the ball with your front arm and taking it early means that you have about two feet less time to get set and swing than you do on the forehand. You must be prepared early to avoid swinging late—and I always tend to be at least a little late.

But I wanted to be able to hit the shot and have the shot. And I wanted it, I said to Howard, because in all of tennis, it was the most beautiful shot. It was formidable because its mechanics were intricate and the timing unforgiving; but, struck properly, it was the embodiment of smoothness and unforced strength. I told him how, a couple of years back, during a weeklong stay in Berkeley, where I was teaching at the University of California's journalism school, I had hit for five mornings with an instructor—a member of Cal's tennis team—at the Claremont Hotel's tennis facilities, with a mind to switching to a two-handed backhand. And though I'd picked up the shot fairly quickly, and couldn't argue with how forgiving it was—you could block with it, take balls late, fight off serves into your body—it felt like I was betraying something. (My ambition? My style? Kirill?) No, I wanted a one-hander. I wanted to get hold of and feel confident swinging a shot that was beautiful. I wanted to have that beautiful shot.

"I *love* that!" Howard declared. "It *is* a *beauty,* no doubt. *Love* that. We will get you the backhand, we *will.*"

49

I arrived on Court 12 for my session with Howard at two the following afternoon, after a morning crammed with hour-long classes devoted to doubles' movement and doubles' strategy (with Coach Scheb), followed by a tennis player's lunch on the fly: yogurt, banana, electrolyte-laced sports drink. Howard was easy enough to spot. He was pushing a hopper piled with new balls toward Court 12's far baseline, and wearing, along with his neatly matching blue tennis shorts and shirt, a spectacular white, wide-brimmed sun hat.

"Are we *ready*, then, Gerry?" he pealed my way. I was to position myself across the net from him at the center of the baseline. He'd hit some balls to my right and have a look at my backhand. I tried to relax my arm and my grip, and hopped in place a little, telling myself this was not an audition—it just felt like one. Howard fed me slow-paced balls in silence. He needed no more than two dozen to glean what afflicted me. He bounded over to my side of the net.

"It's a nice swing, Gerry, a *nice* swing," he began. "When you return next year, you will *have* it. In a few months is my bet."

Then he got down to work. "You *must* initiate," he began,

by which he meant I must get my right foot turned out sideways and prepared to hit a backhand much, much earlier. I had to concentrate on the incoming ball and recognize its trajectory before it crossed the net. I was beginning my set-up (foot swiveled, shoulder turned to brush my chin, racquet back and away from my body) way too late and then rushing my swing to compensate.

"Let me say something, Gerry," Howard said—and would say almost every time he began to say something to me. "I believe, I *do,* that if you get that right—if you *initiate* properly and *every time*—you will have a *beautiful* backhand."

With that, there began an hour of hacking and whacking, my eyes glued to the incoming balls, which Howard sent my way with increased pace as I got better at getting turned early on. I got myself set more readily and comfortably coming in on a ball than having to back up. Part of that—as Kirill recognized early on—was that I hit backhands most cleanly when I took the ball a couple of inches above my bent knees. Balls you came in on were suitably low; balls you backed up on you were going to have to take higher unless you *really* backed up. But it was also (as Howard pointed out) that I had a problem backing up and then getting set in time to transfer my weight forward, from my back foot to my front, as you had to do to hit the backhand properly. I was hitting off my back foot and using little but my arm, netting the ball or leaving it short. Failing repeatedly under the watchful eye of a good teacher, I was once again being made aware of, is a way, maybe the only way, to learn a skill.

I can recall hitting some fine backhands over the course of that hour. What I mostly remember, though, are Howard's reveille-volume pronouncements that followed what seemed like every swing I took:

"Get around, get *around*!"

"Patience. Patience. *Patience.*"

"Look at that! *There* you go! *Look* at that!"

"IN-ISH-EE-AAAAT!"

"Lovely ball."

"Right arm back! *BAL*-ance! *BAL*-ance!"

"Beautiful backhand! *Yes!*"

"Go! Swing it! *Go!*"

"Beauty! *See* that ball! A *BE-YOO-TEE.*"

50

As Howard and I left the court, seeking shade under a tented stretch of lawn nearby where a number of coaches were making small talk or checking their e-mails on their phones, he introduced me to Florian Meyer, who introduced me to a new backhand grip. Florian, it turned out, had been watching us hit. A leading young German coach, he was best known in U.S. tennis circles for his website, OnlineTennis Instruction.com, one of a number of new sites that promised to improve your game through some combination of video instruction and personalized analysis via e-mail. We fell into a conversation in which he suggested that most senior players believe they are hampered by their diminishing athleticism, when the problem was actually a lack of proper technique—a democratic problem, shared by players of all ages. "Learn the proper way to do it," he said, "and then practice it again and again and again, until you can do it, yes?" I felt he had summed up my life in a sentence.

Then he asked me to show him how I gripped my back-hand. I removed a racquet from my bag and wrapped my left hand around it, placing my index knuckle on the top bevel of the grip. "Eastern," I said.

"I find these old terms not very useful," he said. "Eastern, Western, Continental—what do they mean, really?" He had a point, I thought. And I was liking the way his mind worked: In another life he might have been a semiotician. "Let's call the top bevel number one and forget Eastern. And let's call the one next to it not Continental but number two. And let's put your knuckle right at one and a half."

"Right on the edge? Not on a bevel? You can do that?"

"Why not?" The point was to tilt my racquet head up just a bit, "open" it. Florian had seen me hitting too many balls into the net, and even the well-struck ones had just a couple of inches of net clearance. My timing, he said, wasn't precise enough yet (i.e., might never be) to get the proper lift from the more "closed" Eastern, or bevel number one, grip. This little change would provide me with more net clearance without diminishing the spin much, and I thanked him for that and said I would try it.

He then began what I saw was a pitch to sign up for his webinars. Verbal instruction was not enough, Florian said. We needed to see our mistakes on film or video to correct them. I got what he was talking about—I'd benefited, in ways, from Dartfish in Utah and from Brian Gordon's wiring me up in Boca. But I knew I wasn't going to enroll in any online program. I liked real-world coaching. Too much of life, even my life, was already in the hands of software engineers, or someone wanting my attention digitally. If the tennis congress was confirming anything, it was the gratification I took from being personally instructed—urged, admonished, edified, improved—and the warmth I found in the purposeful company of those doing the instructing. Learning was humanistic, as vague a term as I knew that to be. I'm sure there are avatars coming, but not for me.

51

I ended that Saturday afternoon walking to a far court for what was described in the congress program as an hour of movement and agility training. The many courts I passed were filled with senior players, scores of them drilling, and the sight of them, under that illimitable desert sky, afforded me the chance to see myself—and what I was up to—as small, less the solo quester (as I had felt for sure with Brian Gordon in Boca) and more a cog in something turning.

I'd read before flying west of a new study by researchers at the Norwegian University of Science and Technology in Trondheim, who'd been studying fitness and wellness for years. They'd come up with a new concept they called fitness age—essentially a measure of cardiovascular endurance—and their conclusion was that fitness age (which could be younger or older than your actual age, depending on the shape you were in) was a better predictor of longevity than chronological age. A person's fitness age was determined by measuring her or his VO2 max, a measure of the body's ability to take in and utilize oxygen. The researchers had based their study on data gleaned from health questionnaires completed by more than fifty-five thousand Norwegian adults beginning in the 1980s, and from death records. It turned out that if you had a fitness age roughly the same as your chronological age, or higher, you had an 82 percent greater risk of dying prematurely than someone whose fitness age was more youthful than their actual age.

The Trondheim scientists also used the data from the study to build out an online calculator capable of determining fitness age with enticing simplicity: A few simple questions, among them your age, gender, waist size, and exercise regimen. It took me only a few minutes to complete, though when I first got my result, I went back and took the test again just to make sure. My fitness age turned out to be twenty-six.

I was in good shape, very good shape, but then so were all these older men and women with me at the congress—and countless others our age who were seriously physically active. It would turn out, as Gretchen Reynolds reported in the *Times,* that among those who learned of the fitness-age study when it was released was Dr. Pamela Peeke, an assistant professor of medicine at the University of Maryland and, at age sixty-one, a competitive triathlete. She contacted the lead researcher of the Trondheim study, Ulrik Wisløff, with an idea: to study participants in the biennial National Senior Games, also known as the Senior Olympics—thousands of men and women ranging in age from fifty to one hundred who participate in competitions in track and field, swimming, and other sports. Peeke and Wisløff asked all the 2014 Senior Olympic qualifiers to complete the online-calculator form; 4,200 did. The Olympians, it turned out, had an average fitness age twenty-five years lower than their actual age. And, Peeke and Wisløff learned, most of them hadn't begun to get serious about training until later in life. They, like me and my fellow congress attendees, were not so much defying age—there is no such thing—as refusing to believe that growing older entails a growing distance from our active, physical selves. They had more time on their hands; why spend it sitting and waiting for what's next?

I was a little late for the movement-training workshop, and Allistair McCaw was already arraying a couple dozen tennis players along the sidelines and baselines of the court, a few feet apart. McCaw was nearing forty, but still had the physique that twice earned him an award as the most fit South African. He lived in Florida now and trained Olympians, college sports teams, and professional tennis players like the Australian Bernard Tomic in what he called "athletic performance enhancement." His stubble, wraparound sports shades, and crossed-arm coach pose—to say nothing of the Under Armour–clad bod—combined to announce: no nonsense. He pointed me to a spot on one of the baselines, and I jumped in.

There soon commenced an hour of crossover-step shuffling, deep lunging, high-step skipping, hopscotch-ladder drilling, figure-eight sprints around cones. . . . It was hot, and I'd now been on one tennis court or another for close to six hours—not always moving, but mostly moving. Allistair was telling us that "good hip mobility, good footwork, good balance" were the keys to playing better and avoiding injury at our age, which made perfect sense, but I was struggling a bit to maintain focus, and gazing nowhere but down, afraid of tripping. I did register that two or three times he referred to us as "athletes like yourselves," and when all the hopping and sprinting was finally done, and we were sitting where we could in what shade there was near the courts, I approached him and asked him what it was like, a top trainer like himself, drilling aging . . . *athletes?*

"Absolutely athletes," he said, and smiled. His voice off the court was surprisingly soft. "Not like athletes at a university or professional athletes, of course. But look at the commitment you are all making today. That's the commitment of an athlete.

And I will tell you this: I really like coaching you because the motivation is all yours. It's not some parent pushing you. It's not someone who is a fine athlete who believes he doesn't need to work on his performance. You want to improve and are motivated to improve. That's the kind of athlete it's a pleasure to coach."

I strolled to my room and showered, read awhile, then called Barbara before I headed to dinner. She was already in bed—it was nearly eleven back east. She'd spent the afternoon at the Whitney Museum, where she had lingered for a long time at a small show of paintings by Agnes Martin. It was easy for me to visualize them; the color and light in her large, square abstractions were those of the southwest: Martin had painted in New Mexico.

"I loved them," Barbara said. "I think I've always been drawn to art that reveals itself slowly. Something you have to stay with and work to get just means more to me."

I knew exactly what she was talking about.

52

The following morning there was more stretching, and a long workshop in which I worked on my service returns. After lunch Howard looked on as I did volleying drills ("arms *out!*") and then, near the end of the day, hovered as I did backhand drills I'd never done before with Ronald Rugimbana. Ronald had learned the game in Tanzania; had come here to attend Boise State and play for the tennis team; and now, in his thirties, worked for Hewlett-Packard in Boise and coached tennis there. He had me stand at the net in my backhand stance and extend my arms and racquet over to the other side of it as he fed me balls from the sideline and I returned them with the net between my torso and swing—this to build awareness that I must keep my left arm straight and extended away from my body throughout the swing to hit the backhand solidly. Ronald also had me run again and again to my right along the baseline with the racquet firmly held at the throat with my right hand, not firmly gripped in my left. "It might not seem logical," he explained, "since you are left-handed, but you will move more quickly and easily if you move to the backhand with the racquet in the other hand, held out to where you are going, and already back behind your body, where it needs to be"—and he was right, a small revelation.

Ronald then had me pick a *part* of the approaching ball that I would hit with my backhand—inside, middle, outside—in order to keep my eye on the ball as I struck it. "You are lifting your head," he observed. "Why? To see where the ball you hit is going? Your looking cannot change its flight path. It's gone." He would shout which part of the ball I was to hit as he fed it to me, and I would say it to myself as I ran, planted, coiled, and swung. And every so often I would hear Howard from somewhere: "Head *down*! Keep it *still*!"

That last day at the congress ended with ninety minutes of head-to-head play among attendees. The game was a popular tennis one, King of the Court. We were assembled three to a court, sorted roughly by skill level. The king went to the far side; the other two players alternated serving to him. If you won two points serving, you became the king.

The coaches, Howard among them, gathered along the back fences, commenting and motivating as the sun lowered and the air began to cool. I was tired but doing okay enough. There was one point I played I have reason to think about now and then. I served into the deuce court up the T and my opponent, maybe ten years younger and 15 percent better, sliced a backhand to my forehand that landed pretty short. I hit a deep, solid crosscourt forehand that put him on the run. He reached it and sliced another backhand up the line, to my backhand. It sat up, and I put everything I had left into it and drove it crosscourt. It felt good. It sounded good. It looked good, arcing low and laden with topspin. It was—well, a beauty.

It landed an inch or two wide.

"That's a pretty good shot," I heard from behind me. I turned. It was Tim Mayotte, "Gentleman Tim," a tall serve-

and-volleyer on the men's pro tour in the '80s who'd reached the top ten. He was a few years younger than me, with a partnership now in a tennis academy and, on this weekend, a celebrity-coaching gig at the congress. "Right shot," he went on. "Good swing. You just missed it." He smiled and tilted his head. "Tennis."

53 |

The grass at Forest Hills was in better shape than it had been the year before—no weevils—but the evening was chillier than when Kirill and I had first ventured out there to practice. It was the last week of September, two days before John and I were to play our first doubles match at the national grass-court Senior Slam, and he and I had arranged to hit with Kirill and get a feel for the surface I hadn't set foot on for a year, and that John hadn't played on since who remembered when. But John had e-mailed earlier in the day that work would prevent him from making the practice session; Kirill had enlisted his girlfriend, Sandy, to stand in as my doubles partner. They were driving to Queens from Westchester and would meet me. I'd taken the subway from the *Times* and changed into my whites and was waiting for them, warm-up pullover on against the autumn crispness, sitting on a bench alongside the court I'd been assigned, breathing in that summer's-passing scent that grass gives off and absorbing all I could of this place I'd so quickly come to love. A tournament official I'd chatted with on my way to the court had told me that this would be the last Senior Slam at Forest Hills, though he didn't know, or wasn't letting on, exactly why.

Kirill and Sandy arrived soon enough, and while Sandy

stretched, Kirill and I took to the court. After a few minutes of mini-tennis, we backed up to the baselines and began to rally. Kirill was keeping the ball on my forehand, hitting flat and with moderate pace, and immediately I sensed a *comfortableness*: a rhythm coming out of my split step; my knees bending because they seemed to want to; my right shoulder turning and my arms stretching out (the right one) and back (the left); my swing extending fully to keep the strings on the ball as long as I could; my follow-through relaxed and complete enough to be showing Kirill the butt of my racquet handle. Grass and a big-tournament atmosphere were no longer new to me, were no longer making me tight—or so I told myself by way of explaining my quickened calm. Adrenaline was flowing, and confidence. I was seeing the ball early and large. My shots were grass-court-appropriate flat: Topspin wasn't going to add much to the bounce on grass; get the ball to your opponent quickly, with a few inches of net clearance. And soon they were coming off my racquet hard, and Kirill started sending them back even harder. "Good hitting, Gerry!" he shouted after I brought a seven- or eight-shot rally (long for grass, for me) to an end with a ball a good foot long. "Good hitting!"

Sandy joined us on court, and after rallying a while longer, Kirill had us get into a doubles formation, me in the ad court, where I would be playing with John as my partner, and up at the net to begin a near hour of drills: volleying, chasing lobs and switching (sides of the court and who was up and back), chipping service returns and charging the net. Kirill spent a lot of time working on my return game, in particular my backhand slice return, which I would have to hit "inside out"—away from my body and back to the server, not naturally across it and crosscourt—in order to keep the return away from the opposing net player. (There was no way I was going to attempt hitting my backhand drive inside out on a service return in a big national match.) To successfully hit this shot with depth and biting backspin, it was important that I achieve a full shoulder turn—that by the time the serve crossed the net, I be tracking it with my gaze directly over my left shoulder. To get that full shoulder turn, it was important that my left hand stayed soft, my grip loose; a tight grip tightens your arm, which tightens your shoulder, which keeps it from quickly, fully turning. Of course, when a shot is difficult (and any inside-out shot is), you get anxious about it, which has a way of tightening your grip, which tightens your arm . . .

I was struggling with the backhand return, leaving most of them short if they cleared the net at all, and could sense my confidence sagging. As darkness approached and our practice time was drawing to an end, Kirill began serving out wide to my forehand, stretching me. I got to most of them, even as he dialed up the pace. I used his pace, sending my last few shots of the evening back to Kirill flat and sharply angled. I left the court with my heart pounding and my sense I could play on these courts with the best reassured, which, I have no doubt, was Kirill's point in feeding me those forehands. And it helped that, as we were leaving the court, Kirill said, matter-of-factly, as if it were obvious: "You're better, much better, a better player, than you were a year ago."

We headed back to Westchester in Sandy's SUV, Kirill driving, me in the back filling my notebook. At one point Kirill remarked over his shoulder, "You were really angling toward the ball at the end, on those forehand returns out wide. Cutting it off, circling it. Moving in, getting your body into it. Not just sideways, not angling back."

"Huh," I said, more to myself than to Kirill, and jotted in my Moleskine: *Andy Clark. Outfielder problem???*

Andy Clark is a philosopher and cognitive scientist at the University of Edinburgh. He is among the most prominent proponents of what has come to be called embodied cognition, an elusive and controversial theory of mind embraced by a number of psychologists, neuroscientists, linguists, and engineers working in robotics and artificial intelligence. Embodied cognition—and I am simplifying here—posits that we learn not only with our brains but also through our bodies. This isn't to say that these thinkers and researchers believe my left hamstring is a repository of thought or engine of reason. What they do believe—or, anyway, would like us to entertain as they set about trying to say *anything* definitive about what the mind is and how it functions—is that problem solving and task mastery are not just going on in our heads. Sometimes the way we move, say, is helping the brain to get things right and done.

Put another way: There is a man of a certain age on a tennis court, setting off in pursuit of a serve hit wide to his forehand. The accepted understanding of cognition (I am simplifying here, too) is that the brain signals his legs and arms what to do through motor commands after instantaneously creating a disembodied *model* of what is happening: computing and inferring from two-dimensional representations on the retina and collating this with abstract assumptions about the world. Eventually, with practice, the brain gets the modeling right and the body parts get the correct signals and the player gets how to best get to that wide serve and return it. His legs are moving in the proper direction and his arms are stretching just so because the brain told them to.

Which brings us to the "outfielder problem," which I read about in Clark's heady *tour d'horizon* of embodied-cognition theory, *Supersizing the Mind: Embodiment, Action and Cog-*

nitive Extension. Clark's book details numerous examples of what he and his like-minded hypothesizers see as evidence that it's not all in our heads, but rather that as our bodies move through specific, real-world environments, they provide sensory-motor feedback to the brain. Learning, that is, entails a constant feedback loop between what our eyes and limbs are experiencing and what our brains are computing. The study of the outfielder problem that Clark cited struck me as particularly interesting and convincing, perhaps because it was bound to intrigue someone spending lots of time trying to figure out how to move quickly toward an incoming ball and cancel its trajectory.

It was Michael McBeath, a psychologist then at Kent State, who led the study of the outfielder problem. The problem was this: How does a baseball outfielder know where to go to be in the right place, at the right time, to catch a fly ball? (As someone who played the outfield as a teenager, I can testify that it is hard to do: That I *could* do it, passably, was the reason I made the teams I did.) According to mainstream cognitive theory, you compute the initial speed and angle, and you know the ball will go up on a predictable curved and arcing path (there is no motor in the ball to keep it from descending), as you know that it begins to slow (a result of gravitational pull) as it reaches its highest point and then picks up speed again as it begins to descend. Your brain will send a signal for you to run in a straight line and meet it.

Here's the problem: Since the ball is so far from you when it is struck by the batter, you are not really able to *see* exactly where it is headed. And here's what the researchers found when they got a few college athletes to shag fly balls: An outfielder *doesn't* see and then run in a straight line toward the arcing ball. He apprehends the curve of the ball as he begins to move, taking a step with the crack of the bat, and then runs a curved path that mirrors the curve of the ball, his curve "canceling" that of the ball so it looks to him, as he moves, as if the ball is *tracing* a straight line. And he doesn't run at one constant speed: He speeds up and slows down in such a way that the ball *appears* to be moving at a constant velocity through its entire flight. The researchers are convinced—and they pretty much convinced me, too—that there was no pure modeling of parabolic trajectories going on upstairs. Rather, the outfielder's body, his eyes and legs, were in a complex loop with the brain, and together, any number of *embodied* mental adjustments brought the ball to the outfielder's glove.

As such adjustments—*finally*—were bringing my racquet head to a serve out wide. Or so I thought to myself. I pictured it as Kirill, Sandy, and I drove along in silence: me no longer running a straight line sideways, under the illusion that this route was either the quickest or was buying me more time, but moving forward as well as laterally, taking small steps, arriving earlier, and circling more behind the ball to lend my return the power a body stretched fully to the side and off-balance cannot generate. I closed my eyes and saw myself ripping a tough, angled return winner on the Forest Hills grass, my partner John tapping his racquet head against mine as we moved to position ourselves for the next serve coming to him in the deuce court.

In a way, I was engaging in the sort of visualization you're supposed to do in preparing for any game or match (or sales pitch, for that matter): thinking positively, confidently. But more, I'd like to think, I was seeing what constituted *me* in a different way. I'd arrived at a way of living—if only on a tennis court, perhaps, if only for a while—I'd been after for years. I had gotten myself out of my head. I was *embodying* life.

54

John and I planned to meet at the train station in town, take an 11:06 to Grand Central, and catch an uptown 6 and then the E to Forest Hills for our match at the grass-court senior nationals. I got to the station first, and while waiting, read an e-mail I'd gotten from Alexandra. I'd written to her to say how nervelessly excited I was about the match, how different I felt than a year ago, before my anxious singles adventure, and she'd written back: "Singles is a fearsome struggle for independence at best; at worst it is a denial of the other's humanity. But doubles is different. A devoted team can help each other grow so much. You're talking about fellowship, and the delicate, intricate, wondrous balance between autonomy and dependency." I loved how she so unblinkingly glimpsed a tennis court as an arena for inner-life tussle.

John, like me, had a warm-up jacket on over his tennis whites when I spotted him bounding up to the train platform. Summer was all but over. An hour later we were still wearing our jackets, even in the midday sun, walking the noon-crowded, polyglot streets of downtown Forest Hills, looking for a deli where we could get a pregame yogurt and banana. We ate on a bus-stop bench, and John talked about how he and a younger brother—he'd played tennis at Denison in Ohio—had redone two hard courts out in the woods on lakeside property the family owned in Michigan, courts where his father had played; and about how his father had died young, and how he, John, wanted to find a way to spend more time playing summer mornings with his brother and younger family members on those courts by the lake.

Our match was scheduled to begin at 3 p.m., but when we arrived around 1:45, we were told a court would be open a half hour earlier, if we were ready. I was. And I wasn't getting jittery as John and I waited to meet our opponents and be given a court. It was going to be fun. Paul had e-mailed me earlier in the week, and said he might come watch. The vibe at the West Side Tennis Club was friendly, as it had been the previous year, though there was wistful talk about how the senior grass-court championships would be moving elsewhere next year.

All morning, in the moments I had to myself, I had been doing the visualization thing tennis players are supposed to do: imagining John and me winning all manner of points, seeing me nail first serves and punch volleys up the middle, staying focused and positive. We would be the sixty-and-over version of those great lefty-righty doubles teams; teams that forced their opponents each point to confront the differing spins, angles, and ball trajectories created by left-handers and right-handers; teams, as a result, that never allowed those they played against to get comfortable, settle in: Bob and Mike Bryan; Todd Woodbridge and Mark Woodforde ("The Woodies"); Martina Navratilova and Pam Shriver; and John McEnroe and Peter Fleming, who I'd seen play all those years ago at Wimbledon.

I was thinking about McEnroe especially, waiting on the club's crowded veranda, because out across the courts, in the old, ruin-like stadium, the Replacements were doing a sound check—the *Replacements,* those alt-rock pioneers who had rudely crashed on the scene, like McEnroe, in the late '70s, and then mellowed some and peaked, like McEnroe, in the mid-'80s. What remained of the band would be playing a revival-tour concert that night. I heard strains of "Bastards of Young": I'd been crazy for that song. Now they were no longer young, and neither was I. I'd given a cassette tape of their album *Tim* to a short-story writer I had a crush on. It was before I'd met my wife. That was a long time ago. Where was she now, the writer? I was drifting from my visualization.

The announcement of our names on the PA system brought me back to Forest Hills. John and I made our way to the check-in desk, where we were given a court number and a can of balls, and met our opponents. Bill Busiek, trim and beaky, with wisps of gray curling from beneath his pulled-tight tennis cap, was a coaching pro in Marblehead, Massachusetts, and for years had been one of New England's top senior players. Mark Garner was bigger, football big, and together the pair had spent the summer on the New England senior circuit. They'd upset the top-seeded doubles team in the sixty-and-over at Yale, the Senior Slam where I'd spent no time losing to the singles top-seed. They could play.

We warmed up for fifteen minutes, sizing up the conditions (a little breezy) and feeling one another out (they were very good, but we weren't going to be routed). An umpire arrived (this was new!), a woman our age, and flipped a coin. We won and chose to serve. John, with his harder, more reliable serve, would start it off. She, the umpire, would be looking over our match along with one about to begin on the court next to ours. I bounced on the balls of my feet up at the net and spun my racquet around in my hands to keep my hitting arm from tensing up. I told myself that a flutter of nerves—nerves of this kind, just before a match began—was a privilege at my age, and focused on Bill Busiek as he prepared to receive in the deuce court, focused on his shoulders to be precise, which, as they turned, would be first to tell me where John's serve was headed.

John's first serve, up the T, didn't come back. He went on to hold easily. During the brief changeover that follows the first game of a set, I allowed myself the thought that I'd finally won a game at a national senior tournament. Bill served first for their team—a heavily junked-up spin serve, off a wide toss, that arced and hissed like a cartoon curveball. It was murder when he placed it into your body, or up the T, as I would come to know, but in this game I managed a couple of good low forehand returns up the middle. We broke him and were up 2–0.

I failed to hold my serve in the third game, a long game that went to four deuces. Then they held: We were back on serve at 2–2. Then our wheels came off.

John struck a hard spin serve out wide to begin the fifth game—a winner—and the umpire shouted, "Foot fault!" His foot had touched or crossed the baseline before the ball was struck, and the point did not count. John hit his second serve, and was called for a foot fault again: Double fault, point theirs. Twice more in the next three points John foot-faulted. And I could sense something shifting, in that subtle something-in-the-air way it can in a tennis match. John was now a bit rattled, which, in turn rattled me—he was the better player of us two, the one to be counted on. We tried to convince ourselves—with encouraging words and body language—that it was nothing. Our opponents, meanwhile, who just minutes before were in a tougher match than they expected, or so I assumed, now appeared more relaxed and confident. Their energy had risen.

We would lose that game and then the next three, and thus the set: 2–6. The games were close, a couple of them deuce games, and it was more often the case than not that when all four of us were at the net, trading volleys at a point's end, they were simply better, more experienced volleyers: knew how to move together as teammates to close the middle, knew how to redirect balls and wait patiently for putaways. But we'd had a psychological edge back in game five, and lost it.

We didn't fold, though. John held his serve to begin the second set, and hold after hold followed. John had found a rhythm and was serving and volleying with verve, taking returns of his serve back behind the service line and driving his volleys deep up the middle. The points all around were fast and crisp and clean, with few unforced errors. It was tennis at a level I had never played before. I wanted to win, of course, but mostly, on this brilliant afternoon, I wanted the tennis to go on and on. Winning or losing, set two was going to be a matter of just a point here, an inch there, anyway. But to remain if we could so present, so tireless, so alive . . .

In the seventh game of the set I spun a serve up the T at 40–5 that alighted on the chalk before hooking beyond the reach of Bill's stretch backhand. It was my first ace, and it put us up four games to three. And we promptly went up 40–0 in the following game, and had three break-point chances to go up 5–3, and a break would give John the opportunity to serve for the set and force a third. It could go on! But we failed to cash in on any of those break chances—failed to successfully return any of Mark's following three serves. I sliced two backhand returns long. They were no longer putting any serves on my forehand; they had figured me out. They won that game after it went to deuce twice, and won the next two (both of them going to a deuce) to take the set 6–4 and the match.

John and I hugged and we went together to the net to shake hands with Bill and Mark. "Work on that backhand—that's it," Mark said to me as we left the court, and I took it as a compliment. I saw Paul sitting on a bench across the way and waved. He walked toward John and me, ready to mark the day as we mark the days we want to now—with an iPhone snap. John and I put our arms around each other's shoulders, and I smiled: at my friend Paul in his baggy blazer, a steel hook extending from the left sleeve, holding the phone aloft with his still-strong right hand; at the sight of the tennis lawns extending behind him, and the long, fall-coming shadows the players were casting; at the thought of my partner, who had played so well and been a great teammate and (we vowed) would be again; at the thought of my game. I *had* a game. After all the hours and years. And it could and would get better. Could someone be happier in defeat? Some shard of a Richard Wilbur poem, just a couple of words, came to me. Fading and losing would not rob me of my *stubborn joy.*

55

*N*EED TIME TO WORK ON BACKHAND RETURN, I wrote in my notebook—filling a whole page, in big capital letters, underlining it—as Paul, John, and I drank iced tea on the veranda at Forest Hills. The word *time* was scattered through my notebook, as it was in all the notebooks I'd been filling since getting serious about playing tennis. Signposts to remind me that the road was not only difficult but endless; or, better perhaps, the answer—*time*—to the one question I always had: What, at my age, was the best way to keep learning, to get better? I would have to find the time. Time to precisely learn proper techniques. Time to repeatedly practice them, so that they would not break down under the pressure of a match. Time to play more competitive matches and learn to face the pressure. Time to grasp how to better create points, sync up with a partner . . .

But there would be less time for tennis in the coming months. My mother would die suddenly, of a stroke at eighty-five, just weeks after the match at Forest Hills. She had loved me and the life I had made for myself, but she'd frowned on my playing tennis. I would phone her and my father every Sunday morning at nine, and she would ask about Barbara and the kids, and what I was reading. And every Sunday she would bring the call to an end after twenty minutes or so by asking what I would be doing the rest of the day. I would say I'd be playing tennis. If it were summer, she'd reply: "It's too hot." If it were winter, she'd reply: "You're going to be stiff and hurt yourself." Sometimes, whatever the season, she'd say: "You're not so young anymore, kiddo."

Among the many things you are not prepared for when a parent dies—the sight of your mother's lifeless body; the bland banalities, but also the efficiencies, of the funeral business; the long-lost relatives showing up at the memorial mass—there is this: You feel older, weighted by age along with the grief.

On Sundays that fall and through the winter I would drive to New Jersey to visit my dad. I'd tune the radio to Jonathan Schwartz's show on public radio and listen to him play my parents' music—Ella, Sinatra, Tony Bennett, the American Songbook—as I crossed the George Washington Bridge and headed west to the aluminum-sided two-family home where my parents had lived by themselves on the modest first floor for so many, many years. My father and I would eat sandwiches I'd bring from an Italian deli near me in Westchester and watch the Giants play football, and then, at season's end, the NFL playoff games. And when there was no longer any football to watch, we'd take a walk if it was sunny and there was no ice on the sidewalks, or, on cold gray Sundays, just sit and talk in the tidy living room, a room decorated with family pictures, one of my mother as a young bride now set atop the console that encased the television.

My dad would speak of distant things, as those in their late eighties are inclined to do, their long-ago memories bubbling up clear even as they struggle to remember what they had for breakfast. He told me about classes he had liked at Eastside

High School in Paterson, where he never finished (though he would later earn an equivalency diploma), and about learning his way around the USS *Franklin D. Roosevelt,* a new Midway-class aircraft carrier, launched as the war was coming to its end in 1945, the year he was finally old enough to join the navy. He recalled in detail studying for and passing the police exam (a job my mother would never allow him to take), and how he memorized street names and routes during all those years he drove trucks and loaded them and then supervised those who did.

Time speeds up as we age—an illusion we feel as real, especially in our sixties and beyond, however difficult it has been to prove experimentally. Richard A. Friedman, a professor of clinical psychology at the Weil Cornell Medical College, has a theory about this. He suggests that we perceive time as having unfolded more slowly in our younger years because that is when we did the bulk of our learning. "It takes time to learn new tasks and encode them in your memory," he has written. Friedman points to studies showing that the greater the cognitive demands of a task, the longer its duration is perceived to be. We don't sense those years as having flown by because they are crowded with memories like my dad's, memories of learning, memories that can be summoned later in life because their creation was careful, deep, and meaningful. Friedman's advice to the aging is: If you want time to slow down, become a student again.

I would spend Sunday afternoons with my father, and not play tennis matches, but I would still hit with Kirill on Saturdays through the long winter, and join the clinic he ran on Sunday mornings and, sometimes, the one he held on Thursday nights. John and I would make plans to enter the Yale Senior Slam as a doubles team come spring; and Barbara and

I would find ourselves talking more seriously about my retiring from the *Times* and downshifting, easing into whatever phase was next in our lives; and Kirill and I would talk about working on my drive backhand and my backhand volley—one I could poach with, landing firmly on my left foot as I punched the ball—once it warmed up and we got outside again. In the summer, when those afternoons stretched on and on, there would be time enough for most everything.

Acknowledgments

Thanks to:

My former colleagues at the *Times* who encouraged and improved my writing about tennis: Megan Liberman, Aaron Retica, Dean Robinson, Joe Sexton, and Jason Stallman.

My editor at newyorker.com, David Haglund, for keeping me in the tennis-writing game.

My literary agent, David McCormick, who saw a book when I had only a notion.

My dear friends Jennifer Egan and Michael Pollan, for reading a draft and making sage suggestions.

My editor at Scribner, Colin Harrison, for being so attentive and incisive.

My wife, Barbara Mundy, for everything.

About the Author

Gerald Marzorati was the editor of the *New York Times Magazine* from 2003 until 2010. He previously worked as an editor at *Harper's* magazine and the *New Yorker.* He is the author of *A Painter of Darkness,* which won the PEN/Martha Albrand Award for a first book of nonfiction. His writing about tennis has appeared in the *New York Times* and on NewYorker.com.